Praise for
Stop Workplace Drama

"*Stop Workplace Drama* does more than reveal excuses for the inclination to drama in the workplace; it offers a wealth of ideas to improve communication, trust, and leadership that will help eliminate the energy, time, and talent drain that drama creates."
—Stephen M. R. Covey, author of the *New York Times* and *Wall Street Journal* number one best seller, *The Speed of Trust*

"This easy-to-read book is a must have for anyone who leads others and wants to improve the workplace dynamics so your people can enthusiastically say, 'Thank God It's Monday!'"
—Roxanne Emmerich, author of *Thank God It' s Monday!: How to Create a Workplace You and Your Customers Love*

"*Stop Workplace Drama* offers practical ideas to improve communication in the workplace to eliminate power struggles, backstabbing, and office drama."
—Michael Linenberger, author of *Master Your Workday Now!*

"Marlene Chism's no-drama approach is down-to-earth and effective, plus it's communicated with good humor and a very big heart.
—Rick Hanson, PhD, author of *Buddha's Brain: The Practical Neuroscience of Happiness, Love, and Wisdom*

"*Stop Workplace Drama* is filled with fresh strategies to help leaders navigate change, reach their objectives, and create a positive work climate—all at the same time!"
—Jill Konrath, author of *SNAP Selling* and *Selling to Big Companies*

"Any entrepreneur who wants to eliminate excuses and complaints and increase cooperation will benefit by reading *Stop Workplace Drama*."
—Mike Michalowicz, author of the cult-classic, *The Toilet Paper Entrepreneur*

"If you are suffering from negativity in the workplace or your life, and aren't sure how to confront your boss, employee, or family member in a constructive way that initiates positive change, the skills you learn in *Stop Workplace Drama* will blow you away. Marlene's techniques really work, and are more than just mumbo jumbo! She offers solid principles and techniques that, when implemented, will make your environment happier and more productive."

—Sam Glenn, speaker and author of *A Kick in the Attitude*

"Marlene Chism has given the Drama Zone its own zip code! This book is a brilliant approach to halting drama in the workplace—right here, right now—and at every level within the organization. No smoke and mirrors, just real-world tips, tools, and techniques to creating a "no excuses, no complaints, no regrets" workplace. Count me in!"
—Anne Bruce, speaker and best-selling author of more than 14 books, including: *Discover True North, Be Your Own Mentor, How to Motivate Every Employee, Building a High Morale Workplace*, and *Speak for a Living*

"Marlene entertains you on one page and makes you question your intentions on the next. The sage advice in *Stop Workplace Drama*, particularly the culmination of the fulcrum point of change and shift to creator mode, has helped me grow as a leader and inspire our staff to get clarity through the turmoil of growth."

—Ruscell Pavlin, owner and HR director, Therapy Support

"Marlene, where were you 25 years ago when I started my career in the human resources field? The real-life solutions you offer to overcome drama can be applied in a heartbeat. As I continue to coach and mentor individuals, *Stop Workplace Drama* will be in the middle of my desk."

—Pam Mac Morran, senior professional in human resources; former corporate HR director and principal, PDA Search LLC

Stop
Workplace
Drama

Train Your Team to Have No Excuses,
No Complaints, and No Regrets

MARLENE CHISM

WILEY

John Wiley & Sons, Inc.

Published by John Wiley & Sons, Inc., Hoboken, New Jersey.
Published simultaneously in Canada.

For general information on our other products and services or for technical support, please contact our Customer Care Department within the United States at (800) 762–2974, outside the United States at (317) 572–3993 or fax (317) 572–4002.

Wiley also publishes its books in a variety of electronic formats. Some content that appears in print may not be available in electronic books. For more information about Wiley products, visit our web site at www.wiley.com.

ISBN 978-0-470-88573-4 (cloth)
ISBN 978-0-470-94873-6 (ebk)
ISBN 978-0-470-94874-3 (ebk)
ISBN 978-0-470-94875-0 (ebk)

Printed in the United States of America

10 9 8 7 6 5 4 3 2 1

Contents

Acknowledgments

To my friends and family, who love me no matter what my position, title, role, or status. There is great comfort in having deeply rooted relationships. I am blessed to have you in my life.

To my husband, Gerald Chism, who has been with me from day one on my journey of reinvention and who believed in me before I believed in myself. Thank you for providing a solid foundation on which I could continue to grow personally and professionally.

To the team at John Wiley & Sons, Inc., for helping me to realize my publishing dream. Thank you for the opportunity and for your guidance.

To my marketing manager, Jocelyn Godfrey, for your advice, your expertise, and your support. This book exists because of your relationship-building capabilities and marketing savvy. You bring joy to my work.

To my past and present clients for hiring me for coaching, speaking engagements, and consulting projects. Thank you for including me in your world and for applying the Stop Your Drama Methodology in your business and in your life.

My life is blessed personally and professionally because of the quality of people who continue to influence me on a daily basis. I am grateful for those in my life now and for those whom I know I will meet on the journey.

Introduction
We Don't Do Drama Here

The very fact that you are a complainer shows that you deserve your lot.

—James Allen

What Is Drama?

The phrase "stop your drama" gets attention and varied reactions. More often than not, I hear a deep breath with a head nod of recognition from an office manager or business owner who says, "Wow. We need you in our office. We have *tons* of drama." Others react to the word "drama" with a bit of shame, embarrassment, and an attempt to hide any trace of personal or professional commotion. In fact, I was once hired to provide my signature team-building training, but was asked to change the program's name because the meeting planner told me, "We don't want to alert and upset people by using the word *drama*."

Others laugh with recognition and say something like, "My daughter is a drama queen." Another interesting response is "I don't do drama." It's always a red flag to me. I can almost bet that the person who claims not to do drama is the biggest drama queen, a bully, or just completely clueless.

Case in point: While on a recent vacation, I stopped at a little family-owned roadside café for a very late breakfast. Because there were no other customers in the restaurant, I got into a lively and humorous conversation with the owner plus her ex-husband, who was flirting with me, and her mother, who had just told me all about her medical problems. (Yes, they probably could have used some customer service training—but that is beside the point.)

1

After a few minutes, the owner asked me what I did for a living, to which I answered, "I help people stop their drama. You can see what I do by visiting my web site at www .StopYourDrama.com."

The owner responded by proclaiming, "I don't do any drama. I left it behind a long time ago. I'm even friends with all my ex-husbands, including the guy who was just flirting with you."

Then her ex-husband piped up and said, "Well, you do have drama with your ex-boyfriend. Tell her about that!"

That's all it took to initiate stories of stalking, threats, family squabbles, police records, and just about any and all kinds of personal drama you could imagine—followed by the question "What should I do?" As it turns out, this woman did have drama—and a lot of it. She just preferred to deny its existence, or maybe she had become so accustomed to it that she no longer recognized where it was occurring in her life.

As you can see from this example, personal drama can easily become professional drama, even if you don't realize or intend it. This café conversation was not customer-friendly, but because the owner's problems were first and foremost on her mind, she felt that she could bring them out in the open and describe them—in detail—to a complete stranger.

I've had the same experience with massage therapists, nurses, nail technicians, and sales reps—all kinds of professionals who were supposed to be focused on my needs, yet needed a compassionate ear to discuss what was first and foremost on their minds—their own drama. What impacts us personally also impacts us professionally, in both subtle and not-so-subtle ways.

I've also found that the people who have the most drama are often those who are in the most denial, or who simply operate out of a different definition of drama than the one I use in the Stop Your Drama Methodology.

There are reasons, I believe, why people don't want to be associated with having drama. The word *drama*, when used in the context of human relationships, is scary to many. On the personal front, it conjures up images of screaming matches between spouses, or a two-year-old's temper tantrum. On the professional front, drama elicits visions of the workplace bully, a mean boss, power struggles over seniority, backstabbing, over-reacting to change, and office gossip.

All the above definitions and scenarios are representative—or perhaps manifestations—of drama.

In reality, drama reveals itself in all kinds of ways—most of which are so subtle that they are hard to identify until the damage has been done.

Drama can be:

◆ Worrying about whether your upcoming performance review will result in a raise.
◆ The little resentment you have toward your boss.
◆ The confusion and turbulence you feel before making a career change.
◆ Avoiding the difficult conversation, or regretting a decision that has led to procrastination.

Since the source of drama varies and affects so many areas of life, I have developed a definition of it that is more global: *Drama is any obstacle to your peace and prosperity.*

Drama's manifestations always occur because there was a failure to recognize it when it first started. You ignored the subtle innuendo from the indignant co-worker; two years later, you have a workplace bully situation. You allowed your favorite employee to have a key to the office, and now you suspect theft. In other words, these outcomes are the symptoms of drama that have magnified because of a lack of awareness and resulting action.

Have you ever acquired a really bad cold, only to realize that you had truly begun to feel exhausted and run down two weeks prior? Your body had been trying to tell you to slow down, eat right, and get some rest, but you ignored it until you didn't have a choice any longer. You then become so sick that your only options were to rest, or visit the doctor. This is a pretty common occurrence for many of us who feel that we're simply too busy to stop and take it easy.

Or have you ever been managing a team, and instead of addressing the workplace bully, you justified his behavior because he was such a good salesman—only instead of being rewarded for his strength, your company is later slapped with a lawsuit from a disgruntled employee? The signs were there, but you either didn't notice them or didn't act on them.

Drama is like that.

Drama might mean that you ignore the little feelings of resentment you have toward a particularly contentious staff member—until the threat of having to let her go leaves you no other choice but to deal with the circumstances for which you are emotionally, physically, and mentally unprepared. It could also be that you keep ignoring colleagues' and/or customers' complaining and backstabbing. This may well continue until you start losing business, or come face to face with the reality of turnover—and have no other option but to address the drama head on.

The problem in both of these scenarios is that by the time you deal with the drama, it takes a lot more time to fix the problem or get over the damage that has already been done than it would have if you had addressed it sooner. And the more we ignore drama, the more ingrained that habit becomes, until our ability to recognize it is inhibited. We grow numb to it, because we've conditioned ourselves to ignore it.

So, drama is the obstacle to your peace and prosperity. And most members of the business world are concerned primarily with prosperity.

What I have discovered is that in order to flourish in business or in life, you not only need prosperity, you also need peace. Peace allows you to enjoy your prosperity. Having prosperity without peace usually brings a hollow victory; at best, you will gladly give up a big portion of your prosperity to find your peace.

The key, however, is to know that, in fact, you can have it all.

Even if your drama isn't substantial by most people's standards, it may be just enough to disengage your employees from your purpose. According to Gallup.com, "Research by Gallup and others shows that engaged employees are more productive, more profitable, more customer-focused, safer, and more likely to withstand temptations to leave. The best-performing companies know that an employee engagement improvement strategy linked to the achievement of corporate goals will help them win in the marketplace."

A privately owned analytic software company in North Carolina called SAS makes employee engagement a priority goal and a part of their strategic initiatives. As stated on their web site, the action items to implement this initiative are, "To continue to put employees first by investing in both their future through innovation in R&D training and recognition programs, and to continue to recognize employees as the greatest asset in intellectual property enterprise, and treat them accordingly."

It's obvious that stating your purpose is only part of your efforts to maintain clarity for your company; you must also take action on your stated commitments. In addition, if you are thinking strategically, you might have already assumed that this kind of commitment to your employees will be easily tested during tough times. We will talk about how this might occur as we proceed through this journey. Keep in mind that this book's overall goal is to help you clarify your goals and purpose, and create the right mind-set to bring your team with you.

What Is the Obstacle to Your Peace?

An obstacle to your peace could be a number of things—the voice in your head reminding you of past mistakes, concern over losing your job, or a disagreement you had with your business partner. Your obstacle might be the health scare you had when you went for your cancer screening, or your unruly teen who is tattooing and piercing every part of her body. Or, like the café owner, the obstacle to your peace might be a personal relationship problem that has you spewing your problems to your clients. The end result of any of these obstacles could become a prosperity problem—when your customers sense your drama and decide never to return to your business.

What Is the Obstacle to Your Prosperity?

It goes without saying that if you have obstacles to your prosperity, you also will have obstacles to your peace. You'll experience stress—and eventually, that stress will impact your productivity and personal effectiveness.

An obstacle to your prosperity in your personal life might be living above your means in an effort to keep up with the Joneses, or racking up too much credit card debt. Or it could be things you cannot control, such as the rising cost of health care.

Professional obstacles might be the bickering and office gossip going on in the workplace. There tends to be a lot of time wasted complaining in offices—time that could instead be devoted to productivity. An ineffective supervisor who causes turnover will be another obstacle to your productivity. In fact, constantly training new employees to replace the ones who left due to drama can significantly impact your prosperity.

The Society for Human Resource Management (SHRM) has estimated that it costs $3,500 to replace one $8.00-per-hour employee when all costs—recruiting, interviewing, hiring, training, reduced productivity, and so forth—are considered. And SHRM's estimate was actually the lowest of the 17 nationally respected companies who calculated this cost!

Other sources provide the following facts and figures: Employee replacement costs range from 30 to 50 percent of the annual salary of entry level employees, 150 percent of middle level employees, and up to 400 percent for specialized, high level employees!

Despite our ability to amass this kind of information, it's difficult to identify where the real drama lies. Some people assume it's all due to turnover, when in reality it comes from an ineffective supervisor and poor interpersonal relationships.

In fact, the number one reason for turnover is relationship problems with the boss.

You may think the real drama at home is about the fight you had with your spouse, but it's really about all the times you avoided having the difficult conversation, failing to listen or speak your truth to others, or even yourself.

As you can see, drama impacts all of us—both at home and at work. It hampers productivity and inhibits personal effectiveness. And the worst part, of course, is that if you can't spot the drama, you can't stop the drama. Nonetheless, most of us try to fix the symptoms instead of identifying the core issues.

Attempting to make progress without addressing your drama properly is like floundering in a sinking rowboat. You're trying to row to the island called "profits" but denying that there is a leak in your vessel. You can bail water every so often, but doing so only exhausts your rowers. You can blame the boat maker, but that won't stop the leak either. You can row harder and faster and even bring on more rowers, but the water keeps coming in. You can even get angry and hit your teammates over the head with the oars, but this will not plug the leak. Until you identify the real problem—a leak in the boat—you will have more and more drama until you are forced to get a new boat.

The Language

In the above example, I referred to "the island" and "the boat." You will see this analogy often throughout this book. In the Stop Your Drama Methodology and in my team trainings, we use a common language that I call *the language of the island.*

I encourage the use of this language for several reasons. First, learning is easier when you do not feel threatened. Instead of a team member saying, "I am working without enough resources and with an incompetent team," the person can say, "We are using a row boat when we need a speed boat, and everyone is beating each other with the oars." This way, you can use the power of creativity—which you will learn about in

Principle 8—and focus on the problem instead of casting blame and pointing fingers.

A second reason for using this new language is that it helps to create a cohesive bond and eliminate assumptions. Instead, it fosters curiosity and open communication. Third, using this new language activates the right side of the brain—where innovation and problem solving interact with insight.

A neuropsychologist and neurobiologist by the name of Roger Wolcott Sperry won the 1981 Nobel Prize for his work studying how the hemispheres of the brain differ and are responsible for managing certain types of skills and tasks. Since then, researchers and educators have been developing means by which to activate areas of the brain, such as the creative right side. In addition, some business schools are now seeking out "right-brained" individuals who may have additional creative problem solving skills not so commonly found in linear thinking. The idea behind this is that creative types can think on the fly and come up with innovative solutions to business dilemmas. I similarly encourage the use of such creative language in my methodology, so as to activate the area of the brain that can assist in solving bigger problems.

The point is that this language provides a new sense of freedom, camaraderie, and creative problem solving while discussing and exploring otherwise very sensitive and complex issues, both personally and professionally. In keeping with the island terminology language, we use some of the following common terms in this book.

Common Terms

Lost in the fog

Stuck on the rock

Shoveling coal in the boiler room

Navigating the ship

Leak in the boat

Getting to the island

As you can see, some of these terms have implied definitions. "Lost in the fog" clearly hints at a lack of vision or a sense of confusion. "Shoveling coal in the boiler room" implies working long and hard without a purpose or realizing the end result, only to keep things going. This is in contrast to "navigating the ship," which means being on deck with clear vision for what is ahead. A "leak in the boat" occurs when you have negativity, wasted time, or other distractions preventing you from navigating effectively, wherein you are losing energy, momentum, and productivity. "Getting to the island" means achieving and reaching your goal.

The Drama versus Your Drama

Now you have an idea of the language and the definition of drama (any obstacle to your peace or prosperity). There is, however, one more distinction worth mentioning: *the* drama versus *your* drama.

The drama is the situation. *Your drama* is how you react to it. Therefore, while you may not be able to stop *the* drama, you certainly can stop *your* drama. In other words, you may or may not be able to control or change the circumstance, but with some training, you can learn to manage—and alter—your response.

One of my favorite quotes on this concept is by Vivian Greene: "Life is not about waiting for the storms to pass. It is about learning to dance in the rain."

Most people do not know how to separate the drama from your drama; however, after reading this book, you will be a pro at recognizing what you can control and what you can't. You will realize that you may not be able to stop the rain, but you can learn to navigate the ship even in a storm—with the right equipment, maintenance, and planning.

What Comprises Drama

When trying to identify the common elements in drama, you will always find at least one of three common elements if not all three: a lack of clarity, a relationship issue, and/or resistance. In addition, you may also see any combination of the other five principles in the Stop Your Drama Methodology. These principles work as a system rather than a step-by-step linear process. When you make a shift in any one of the eight areas, the impact will have a ripple effect. However, you will always be able to identify at least one of the three core components immediately.

1. A lack of clarity (which I also refer to as *fog*)
2. A relationship issue
3. Resistance

These three components will be addressed specifically in Chapters 1, 5, and 7. In addition, we will see how these components overlap in examples throughout the book.

When you experience drama, three questions to ask yourself are:

1. Where am I unclear?
2. What is the relationship component?
3. What am I resisting?

Once you are able to identify how clarity, relationships, and resistance negatively impact your business, you can effectively create a quick solution to help you navigate positive change.

How Do You Use This Book?

If you own a professional practice or operate a business, this book is for you; it will help you both personally and professionally. If your team suffers from drama, you will immediately recognize areas where you either need to increase your own leadership abilities or hand over some of your duties to someone with the skills that you lack.

If you are relinquishing peace and profits to coddle or please an employee who is not contributing to the company's greater good, this book will force you to tell yourself the truth about your motives and real commitments.

If your business is fantastic but your personal life is in shambles, you will be able to use these principles to make significant personal changes that will add to your overall sense of well-being and joy.

If you have conflicting wishes, Principle 2 will introduce the concept of the integrity gap and teach you how to notice when you are getting off course.

This book will help you solve problems pertaining to your business and to your life as well. The principles are universal and apply to individuals, whether they're simply living their lives, running a company, or building a successful team.

Life does not occur in compartments. Whatever impacts you personally will leak into your professional life, and vice versa. That is why this book is full of examples that cover business-related case studies or situations as well as personal ones. This book is for everyone from practice managers to sales directors to company leaders. You'll learn a full methodology with eight universal principles, each of which is accompanied by many practical tools and exercises to help you distinguish the drama from your drama—thereby allowing you to stop your drama, and acquire peace and prosperity.

However, I can almost hear what many of you might be saying as you read through these chapters: "I do what I can with the power I have, but the reality is, I don't own this business."

If that is the case, I understand that you are in the middle in a very real sense. And I feel your pain.

Still, you will get some encouragement here, and you'll be able to see how you can facilitate change when you realize how to become crystal clear on your own life and objectives. I will show you how to focus on what you can control versus what you cannot control, and how to use this newfound sense of clarity to face your fears, prevail over drama, and make substantial changes.

You have much more power than you know.

The one with clarity navigates the ship. If there's drama in your office, I can guarantee there is someone who understands the situation better than you. It might be the star employee who gets her way with the boss at your expense. It might be the troublemaker who is determined to undermine everyone else to make herself look good. If you are the one with the problem, then look for areas where you might need to clarify your communication, illuminate your expectations, or enforce a boundary. Gaining a sense of clarity will help you align your decisions with your values—as well as your company's mission and values—instead of basing them on a fear of confrontation or the need to please or control other people. When you feel like you are shoveling coal in the boiler room to keep the ship going, getting clear will help you step back on the top deck and see things in a different light.

You will hear me say this over and over: If you are afraid of your boss, this book will give you the courage to face that fear. If you are keeping things from your boss, you will look inward to ask yourself where your commitment truly lies. If you are letting the queen bee run the show, you will be forced to face the truth and ask yourself what you are afraid of losing or who you are trying to please—and at what expense. Why are you avoiding the authentic conversation? What are you hiding? What are you afraid of facing? Why are you stuck? What are you resisting?

If these questions stimulate you, that's very exciting; it's a sign that you are prepared for an excellent journey. If, however, these questions make you nervous or your knees go weak, hold on for a moment. My suggestion is for you to read this book first, then give it to the owner, the doctor, or the partner—whatever their title, or whoever this person may be. After you've both read the book, get together for a planning session to create a vision for your workplace, business, or practice. Or call me, and I'll come out for a session to get everyone rowing together.

No matter what your title or position, it takes courage and wisdom to act upon these ideas.

As you read, you will uncover some exciting opportunities. However, I must warn you in advance: This book is intended to make you think, to light a fire in the boiler room of your business, and to ignite the fuel that moves you forward. The process may even make you angry, as you start to realize what is out of alignment and how you want it to change.

You may think you are crystal clear once you get angry enough to speak your truth, but wait before you act on that energy. Here's why: Anger is not clarity—but it can be the momentum that gets you there. Don't go telling off your nemesis, declaring your resignation, or blowing the whistle just yet. Be willing to merely observe before you straighten everything out. I promise that you will thank me later—even if you are a bit uncomfortable at first.

Anger and frustration can actually be very useful emotions. As *The Dance of Anger: A Woman's Guide to Changing the Patterns of Intimate Relationships* author Harriet Lerner says, "Anger is a signal and one worth listening to." If, after reading this book, you suddenly become incredibly frustrated with your business, position, or circumstances, remind yourself that this is exactly the new perspective you need in order to facilitate change. You may need to let a few people go, hire a few more, shift positions—or perhaps close up shop or leave your current position to find something that's more closely aligned to your newfound clarity.

If you think you already know everything there is to know about drama and clarifying your perspective—or you are looking for evidence that I'm wrong—then just save yourself some time and use this book for kindling. That will spare you from the temporary internal drama that you will feel with the newfound awareness that something needs your help in order to change, and will enable you to go on with your business and pretend that everything is okay . . . that is, until it isn't okay any more.

Denial only works for so long before all paths eventually lead to Rome. Even if you haven't reached that point yet where your mind has had enough of the drama, your body ultimately will tell you when you've reached your limit. The headaches, the insomnia, and the heartburn will eventually make you aware that something needs to change—and soon.

Now you get to choose what to do today: Will you resist, or are you willing to seek the change that is currently beckoning you ahead?

Which leads us to the real question that will determine your success in implementing the Stop Your Drama Methodology: Are you willing?

Are you willing to be courageous? Are you willing to speak up? Are you willing to wait in uncertainty, to see things differently, and to look inside yourself? Are you willing to make internal changes? Are you willing to risk becoming angry as you discover what needs to change?

If you are willing, then I can guarantee that some magic will happen. You will see the importance of willingness when you read Principle 7 and learn about the Fulcrum Point of Change. You will see why stubbornness will keep you shoveling coal in the boiler room instead of navigating the ship to the island called customer service, business success, profitability—or any other island you seek. Once you have stepped up on the deck and seen the vision, you can no longer rest in the justification of "that's the way it's always been" or "there's nothing I can do"; nor will you be able to sacrifice yourself to the lower level, shoveling coal in the boiler room.

You will live a different life and on different terms. Get ready for an exciting, life-changing and business-changing, transformational journey that I call "The 8 Steps of Empowerment."

Chapter 1

Clear the Fog

*If confusion is the first step to knowledge,
I must be a genius.*

—Larry Leissner

A few Novembers ago, I was experiencing a lot of internal drama over one particular dilemma: Who should I invite to Thanksgiving dinner? My opposing influences came from all areas of the family. One relative called to tell me that if I invited another particular person, then his wife would not come because she was offended by something that person had said during the previous Thanksgiving. Another called to tell me that if I didn't invite this same person, it would make Thanksgiving the most miserable one ever.

It was becoming so difficult that I considered not having Thanksgiving at all. I was struggling and frustrated.

It doesn't matter if you are under pressure in your personal life or simply can't get your team to follow your lead. The same truth remains in both cases: When you struggle, you also experience frustration.

Here is how the cycle usually goes: You may try to figure out who or what is standing in your way professionally. At first glance, it may seem like it's your trouble-making employee. You tell yourself that if this person would just straighten up, all would be well with the world.

If your small business is struggling, you may think you don't have the knowledge, skills, or resources to make it a success. Maybe you don't understand marketing, aren't skilled at managing others, or have a staff of two and really need four to get where you need to go.

Eventually, you come to the conclusion that the reason you are stuck is because there is someone who does not support, agree with, or understand your decisions. It could be your boss or your colleagues. It could be your employees. It also might be that your personal life has so much drama that you can't focus.

There are a million and one potential excuses as to why you are frustrated, stuck, and not getting what you want, but there is only one real reason: You are unclear. You have fog that is clouding your vision.

The premise of the first Stop Workplace Drama principle, *Clear the Fog*, is as follows:

1. The one with clarity navigates the ship.
2. Clarity can change any situation.

Once you are clear in your business, you are in charge. You attract the right people to your team. They are working toward the same goal. They are motivated. You become excited. You make decisions that are in agreement with who you are and the values that you hold dear. Your choices support and work in harmony with other parts of your life.

The author of *The Five Dysfunctions of a Team: A Leadership Fable,* Patrick Lencioni, states that "A friend of mine best expressed the power of teamwork when he once told me, 'If you could get all the people in an organization rowing in the same direction, you could dominate any industry, in any market, against any competition, at any time'" (Lencioni 2002, viii).

The really cool thing about this first principle—*Clear the Fog*—is that it works as easily in your personal life as it does in your business. Once you become clear in both of these areas, you won't always feel the need to make sure that everyone understands your decisions. You won't spend as much time worrying about what other people say you should do, or beating yourself up for what you should have done. You will make your decisions based on who you are and what values you hold dear, instead of trying to please, manipulate, or rescue others from their own drama.

Let me get back to my Thanksgiving dinner story so you can see how this works. After the initial dread and frustration I experienced over my inability to meet everyone's needs in regard to whom I should invite to the meal, I finally got silent and did a little meditation and journaling—something I often do when I experience a lack of clarity. Suddenly, it came to me: It is my house. I will invite everyone. I did not have to get permission or agreement.

However, this did mean that I had to be okay with the fact that some people would simply not show up. Instead of taking this personally, I decided I would act on my clarity. I remained neutral, and let everyone make decisions about their attendance based on their values instead of my wishes or manipulation. I made it perfectly clear that I intended to have a very peaceful and harmonious Thanksgiving. I told my family and friends that everyone was invited, and if that didn't work for them, I would honor their decision not to attend. I also said that since it was my house, I had the freedom to ask anyone who was not in alignment with my vision to please leave if I sensed any trouble.

The result? It turned out to be the best Thanksgiving I have ever had. My clarity eliminated the drama. I got what I wanted: a peaceful Thanksgiving. The icing on the cake is that everyone attended—and *they all got along.*

The Fog

Let's define what the fog is and what it does.

Everyone knows how exciting it is when you start working toward a new goal. However, somewhere between the first steps and the end result the process becomes difficult. The reason for this is usually because someone on your team is unhappy, and, instead of focusing on the island you are trying to reach, you're now concentrating on pleasing the one person who is upset. Your focus has shifted because you became confused about your number one priority. This is an example of how losing clarity forced you off course because of a conflicting desire or unexpected reaction from someone who has the power to influence you. Or you lose momentum because you start focusing on all the hard work it takes to move forward. Negativity sets in, and now you and your team are no longer motivated.

The fog here is your inability to focus and your lack of willingness to see the bigger picture. Occasionally, you might have two desires that do not align. For example, your desire for free time is competing with your desire to finish a project, so you procrastinate and start drifting aimlessly.

The fog is any distraction or division that clouds your vision and threatens your commitment. When you are in the fog, you feel confused instead of motivated.

In short: Any time you lose focus and your level of commitment diminishes, you are in the fog—and you are splintered. You become what I refer to as *double-minded*.

Though visions and goals are often the first steps toward achieving clarity, there must be something more to sustain it. To keep yourself clear, you must have a strong "why" that supports your goals. This will come from developing your set of core values because, in the difficult times, these are what will lead you out of any fog that threatens your success.

If you aren't sure what your core values are, you may need to work on defining them. You might need to do a bit of soul searching to discern what most matters to you and/or your organization. What principles do you want to live by, no matter what happens around you? What values will you never sacrifice? Once you are aware of your core values, you can set more satisfying goals—goals that support these values. We talk more about this later when we discuss in detail how you can begin to gain clarity.

When I observe people, I often notice that conflict exists because their lives are splintered. They are not quite clear in some area of their life or business.

In the entrepreneurial world, I have had the pleasure of meeting and networking with a lot of "solopreneurs" who just can't seem to make it because they keep changing directions. They put the cart before the horse; they worry about "how" before figuring out the "what"; or they keep waiting for someone else to encourage them instead of believing in themselves and their vision. They seem to be seeking some kind of guru to answer questions that only they can be responsible for. They too lack clarity on what they need, and they are operating in a fog.

I also have had the advantage of working with leaders in the corporate world who are frustrated because they try to lead without having any kind of vision. It's hard to motivate a team when all the work is focused on the drudgery of the everyday grind instead of the success of arriving together at a worthy goal—one that is supported by solidly defined core values. Because of the fog, these leaders are only able to see what is right in front of them, instead of the island in the distance that would beckon them to row more effectively and energetically.

Of course, none of us is perfect, and most goals are not achieved in a linear fashion. There are other factors that challenge us and throw us off track—things like our personality traits, habits, or wiring. Have you ever noticed that some of the things that come naturally to you—such as your particular gifts and hidden talents—can also be the cause of the drama that holds you back? The following are some potential gifts and personality types/traits that have the potential to deter your success.

The Idealist

The highly idealistic leader is often crystal clear in the beginning and good at motivating others. However, she finds it difficult to keep the momentum when the going gets tough. If the journey turns out to be more difficult than first imagined, procrastination will set in—and then come the justifications as to why it's not a good time to move forward. She starts out with one oar and a rowboat with no map, when what she really needs is a yacht and crew to achieve her goals. Her idealism initiates unrealistic expectations for her team, which ultimately leads to disappointment. The challenge for the idealistic person is to see the bigger picture and know what is really required before expending energy convincing others to move forward without enough resources or commitment.

The Creative Genius

Maybe you are a creative genius who—like so many other creative geniuses—is easily distracted. The sparkling island calls to you, and as a result, you have 50 irons in the fire and your energy is all over the place. You want everyone to catch your vision, yesterday—and you want your employees to antici-pate what you are thinking before you let them know, even though your vision changes along with your moods and the weather. Ask yourself if your creativity is contributing to the prosperity of your company—or is your creativity the cloud that fogs your vision?

A colleague of mine, Angela B., worked for a creative boss, the owner of an international travel and tour group. According to Angela, her boss's creativity almost drove her crazy before she finally threw in the towel.

"His mind-set changed daily with at least 10 new ideas. He was extremely indecisive, and therefore, the team lacked direc-tion," Angela recalled to me.

Often, entrepreneurial and creative types do not understand how to balance their genius with the need for structure and clear communication. Angela explained:

"We were organizing an athletic event in Europe for 200-plus athletes and he needed to sign the contracts with different hotels. These contracts were very long, and he never took the time to sit down and read all of the pages (and he didn't trust me or his other assistant to do this properly). It took more than three months to finally get his signature, and I had to save his reputation over and over again so we wouldn't lose the reservations. His excuses for not signing were:

Let's wait and see what the Euro (exchange rate) does.

I don't know if the sizes of their beds are comparable to
    U.S. beds. We should check into that first.
I have to do two million other things; signing these
    contracts is not important."

Angela always felt that her work was never good enough.
She felt incompetent because no matter what project she was
working on, another project would take priority at the drop of a
hat. She said, "It was also difficult to accomplish administrative
work such as organizing files and filing taxes because that was
last on his list of priorities. It felt like we often had our heads in
the clouds instead of getting real work done."

If you are a creative genius, your gift could cloud your vision
when you hire a team. Look at it from your employees' point of
view. You may be more committed to being creative than to
achieving your stated goals. This will cause a division, and may
tempt you to blame the team instead of clearing the fog by
adjusting your patterns to accommodate your goal. Imagine
working for someone on a big project into which you have
poured your heart and soul; then one day, your boss comes in
and says, "Scrap that project. I have a new and better one for you
to work on."

While this kind of creativity can potentially be something
very positive, it can drive your team members crazy because
they never feel a sense of completion. This kills their motivation
and leads to turnover. Not only do they not get to complete the
tasks they begin, they also miss out on getting any recognition
for their skills and accomplishments. They will never know if
what they were doing would have made the difference. They
bought into the vision you introduced, only to have their
horizon shifted 180 degrees midsail.

This kind of leader often forgets that people want to work
from a larger purpose—not just for a paycheck or to complete
each willy-nilly (if sparkly) task that crosses his mind. The
creative genius's challenge is to consider the entire team's feelings, instead of being addicted to the adrenalin of her own
creativity and getting lost in the fog of self-absorption.

The Peacemaker

If you are a peacemaker, you simply love people. You don't want to upset anyone or make anyone unhappy. However, without knowing it, your need to please others or benefit others keeps you confused about your own mission. You may be unaware of your unconscious needs and motives. You keep the peace, hold your tongue, and rescue others—often at your company's expense.

The outcome is that, as the peacemaker, you often end up feeling a sense of resentment because others never appreciate your sacrifices. Though you were unaware of this expectation, you come to anticipate something in return for your benevolence. When you don't receive anything, you tend to feel hurt and insecure about your leadership capabilities.

An extreme case of this might be when an executive assistant is sentenced to prison for tax evasion, along with her boss, because she knowingly assisted him in hiding his malpractice. In many cases, you don't hear about the peacemaker in the news because she doesn't make a ripple. However, she still facilitates drama by not being clear on her responsibility to speak up regarding necessary change.

Clarity means having the courage to speak up—even when it is challenging—and ridding yourself of the justifications that keep you in your comfort zone.

The Analytical

A friend of mine recently told me about a mountain biking adventure she had hoped to take, which never came to fruition. She had accompanied two of her friends to the mountains to camp out, with the intention of riding up and down a peak in the North Cascades of Washington the next day. During that afternoon, however, one of the friends decided he should overhaul the gears on his bike. He tinkered with them, analyzing to make sure they were running optimally, rearranging pieces over and over again, until one key element of the bike broke. The trip was aborted because his bike no longer worked—and my friend was extremely frustrated.

Perhaps you are one of these analytical types of people who tend to think things through. The problem is that you often overthink and get stuck on the rock called "how." You drive everyone crazy twisting everything over and over in your mind, playing out various scenarios, without ever taking action.

If the above description sounds like you, then you must train yourself to understand that "what" always comes first, "who" always comes second, and "how" always shows up after you know what and who. If you get too stuck on "how," the fog will eventually roll in again—thereby confusing everything.

The challenge for the analytical is to gain clarity by inviting others' viewpoints and implementing key ideas while discarding what doesn't work—instead of getting consumed with how it's going to get done.

So—Which One Are You?

You probably see yourself in one or more of these examples. Whether you tend to get overwhelmed by unrealistic expectations, become easily distracted, or get stuck on the rock, it all boils down to a need to gain clarity so that you can move forward.

The Power of the Leader

If you are a sales director, practice administrator, or supervisor, then you are in a position of leadership. The same is true if you are a business owner with a staff of employees, a department head, or even a parent. Therefore, as a designated leader, you have a lot of power and influence in the workplace. Here's something that may be difficult to hear, so take a deep breath: If you have drama in your office, you are the person who is responsible for navigating in the fog.

If you were clear, you wouldn't:

◆ Hide information.
◆ Avoid facing the problems.

- ◆ Feel one thing but do another.
- ◆ Give up your values to gain others' approval.
- ◆ Make excuses about your performance.
- ◆ Blame the situation for your drama.
- ◆ Shift direction without considering how it will affect your staff.

Do you see yourself in any of these examples? If so, then do you recognize that you are responsible for part—or even most—of the current drama?

The good news is this: To increase your power, all you have to do is eliminate the fog. Your vision has to be so clear and inspiring that no doubt exists as to who is in charge and in which direction you are going.

Confusion will inevitably lead to drama. A leader who lacks clarity will drive his or her team crazy and eventually create more drama than you can imagine.

Do you feel, for instance, that your team lacks motivation? If so, figure out if you are guilty of changing your mind in the middle of what you once deemed an important assignment—complete with deadlines and priorities attached to it. Your people gave up their lunch to get it done. They faced their fears of impending change. They spent overtime trying to figure out how to come up with the resources to complete the job, and they listened to your analysis paralysis. Then one day, you saw another sparkling island and told everyone to drop what they had been sweating bullets over for the last three months because you had decided it no longer mattered. Not very inspiring, and not a great way to develop trust, either. One of every human being's underlying needs is a feeling of certainty. When you keep changing your mind with no advance warning, you elicit a threat reaction from your employees and colleagues.

As a creative person myself, I too have been guilty of too much excitement, changing my mind, and starting new projects—until one new assistant quit and called me unstable.

As much as it hurt—and even though she was not necessarily a gifted communicator—I got it, and used it as a lesson.

When you are the one in charge, changing the rules feels okay because you still have some control and a sense of certainty. However, those in support roles can lose motivation when you're constantly changing your mind—unless you communicate and keep them in the loop, and take their feedback into account.

If your group endures petty arguments, disagreements, backstabbing, and power struggles, ask yourself if you are guilty of avoiding team meetings that would serve to update everyone on the new decisions and direction of the company, and consider their input.

I'm sure you could find very good reasons for avoiding meetings. Let's look at a few of them:

◆ I don't have time.
◆ Meetings just turn into gripe sessions.
◆ Not everyone can be there at the same time.
◆ They always take longer than expected.
◆ I'm not good at holding a meeting.

We will talk more about why to have team meetings in Chapter 2, but for now, let me just tie this wisdom in with some familiar connections. In his book, *The 7 Habits of Highly Effective People*, author and management expert Stephen R. Covey would say you need to "sharpen the saw" (Covey 1989, 287). There's also an old proverb dating from before 1732 when it was originally recorded that says, "A stitch in time saves nine." This proverb initially meant that a little effort made now may prevent further chaos later, and was later used by English astronomer Francis Baily in his journal as a means of explaining how he kept his boat on course in the middle of the stream. Everyone may have a different way of explaining the need to invest the time now in order to prevent chaos later—as you would do in a meeting. My saying is that you need to plug the leak.

These reasons why you don't have weekly meetings are really just excuses. While excuses tell you what is happening and why, they never serve to plug the leak. In fact, if you ignore the leak, it will often grow until it sinks the boat.

A leak occurs when we are stuck in the fog so long that we hit a rock or can't see our own mechanical problems. The drama then becomes more than just confusing; it essentially destroys any forward progress we try to make.

You have probably already figured this out, but I'm still going to drive the idea home. All drama has one thing in common: a lack of clarity. So how do you identify this?

- Constantly changing directions
- Conflicting desires that hamper productivity
- Confusion
- Not knowing who the boss is
- Failing to enforce the rules
- Instability
- Insubordination
- Incongruent behavior
- Constant misunderstandings
- Lack of boundaries
- Resentment
- People pleasing and manipulation
- Analysis paralysis
- Waiting for everyone to understand and agree

Any type of discord, abuse, confusion, or game-playing always boils down to a lack of clarity. You will know that wherever drama is, clarity is not. When you are clear, life is good and you are on the top deck; you're motivated by the vision, instead of down in the boiler room shoveling coal.

Who Is on the Top Deck?

If you are a business owner who is constantly covering for some incompetent employee, your employee is the one who is on the top deck. If you are a leader who is allowing your boss to manipulate you or treat you like a doormat, you have lost your insight on who you are and how you want to be treated.

If there is a drama queen in your office who stirs the pot, then I think we both know who is navigating the ship—and it's not you.

Are you beginning to see a pattern here?

There have been so many times when I've witnessed business owners making decisions out of a need to please a prima-donna employee or pot-stirring staff member, rather than addressing the issue and risking upsetting the employee. The owner often stays silent at the expense of the team—or even at the expense of profits.

For example, I once worked with a business owner who was continuing to keep and pay an employee who was lazy, failed to show up to work, and not contributing in any way to the bottom line. The owner's excuse for keeping her was all about the employee's problems, rather than about the business's vision and mission. There were always excuses: "Well, she's had some rough times lately" and "I don't think she could find employment anywhere else." Now, there's really no problem here if the business owner is happy with this arrangement.

If this is the case, I would say to this business owner, "Rescue at your heart's content, if this is your vision for your life. Though you may have lots of peace, I can guarantee that running your company in this way will impact your productivity."

Remember: Drama is any obstacle to your peace and productivity. As a leader and a business owner, you must always be on the lookout for anything that threatens to impede this peace and prosperity.

I have to admit that I was shocked at this particular owner's lack of awareness and clarity about her vision for her own business.

Who was navigating here? Who was on the top deck? Obviously, it was the employee. The business owner had all kinds of reasons for keeping her on board, mostly in the name of maintaining a sense of peace or rescuing someone she considered incapable. However, this owner was not even considering how this rescuing behavior was creating a leak in the boat and impacting her organization's productivity and prosperity.

The simple fact here is that there is a justification going on. The owner would rather go to the island called "pleasing everyone else" than to grow in her leadership skills and risk losing her employee's approval. Once again, we see the fog of distraction or ulterior motives at play.

There are many benefits of gaining clarity. Doing so will bring you peace, save you time and energy, and can change any negative dynamic in your personal or professional life.

CLARITY GIVES YOU PEACE

Remember that I said wherever drama is, clarity is not? All drama involves a lack of clarity, which in turn always brings you peace. When you are at peace, your directives are clear.

Even if you are faced with some dirty work or interpersonal conflict, you can endure it gracefully. Even if there are disagreements and misunderstandings, your door is open when your employees are ready to come around. You have no need to make excuses or please the wrong people. You are clear.

GETTING CLEAR SAVES TIME AND ENERGY

Once again, understanding this principle will help you speed up your decision and keep you from wasting time trying to figure out why someone else is doing what they are doing. You also won't expend valuable energy on blame and resentment and get sucked into more relationship drama. It is extremely important that you get crystal clear on your intentions, objectives, and personal values.

HOW CLARITY CAN CHANGE ANYTHING

It doesn't matter what kind of drama you have; clarity can clean it up. As I said before, drama in your personal life will eventually spill over professionally—even if it seems at first like they are separate issues. Let me share with you a more personal example to help you to see that cleaning up drama personally will impact your career advancement, your productivity, and your sense of well-being, and how the three core components comprise drama.

I had the recent opportunity to be a guest expert on a local radio show where people call in with their questions. I was answering most questions on the air, but one fellow got me on a private line and told me about his issue.

Joe lived in Illinois, and was recently divorced from Patty, his wife for more than 10 years. According to Joe, the divorce was pretty messy. Several months after the divorce, Joe got another job that required him to move 400 miles away from Patty and their two boys. Patty let Joe take the kids out of Illinois once, but then decided she wasn't going to do it anymore. As a result, Joe was divided because he really loved his kids and wanted to be present in their lives, yet he also wanted to excel in his new position 400 miles away. In his way of thinking, it was his ex-wife holding him back. She became the obstacle to his peace.

Out of anger, Joe ended up reducing his child support, and then Patty bucked up even more. Now you are starting to see an example of how the relationship component comes into play in this particular situation. Patty would not meet Joe halfway and was not going to let him see his kids at all because, according to Joe, Patty thought it was way too far.

As I listened to Joe, I could sense his frustration and his worry. I asked Joe, "What do you really want?"

Joe said without any hesitation, "I want to be a good dad to my kids."

Then Joe got distracted by the island called "Why is she doing this to me?" (Can you see the wasted energy and time?)

"Why is she doing this to me?" Joe asked.

"I don't know, because I am not her," I responded.

"But . . . why do you think she is doing this to me?" he continued.

When you look at this dialogue, you can see how easy it is to become locked into drama and storytelling. The fact is that even if I had a good idea about why this was happening, I am not Patty. Even Patty herself might not even know why she's doing what she's doing. When there is underlying hurt, hidden resentment, and unresolved fear, all kinds of drama is bound to surface—and Joe was getting his fair share of it. You can probably imagine how this kind of stress would eventually impact Joe on his new job if he didn't find a way to peacefully resolve his situation. Can you see how Joe might be tempted to talk about his problems with his clients, or how Joe might use this problem as an excuse for poor performance? Personal drama negatively impacts personal performance and spills over into the workplace.

In order to clear Joe's distraction, I asked again, "What do you want?"

Remember how I said before that the reason we don't get what we want is we either don't know what we want or we become distracted? Distraction that impacts personal performance or stands in the way of your highest intention is always an issue of clarity. Joe was consistently distracted by his attempts to figure out his wife. In reality, the best person to ask about this was Patty herself. If Joe wasn't willing or able to have this dialogue, he could still get clear about his values and long-term goals about being a good father to his kids, and gaining a sense of clarity on these values would drive him to different—and likely, more constructive—behaviors and interactions with his ex-wife. This clarity could prevent him from acting on impulsive behaviors and mind-drama with his ex-wife, which could impact his kids in the long run. To make sure Joe understood his own goals, I asked him a big question: "What do you want? In other words, what is the outcome you desire?"

"To be a good father to my kids, which means seeing them on a regular basis," he replied.

I asked, "Will your ex-wife let you see your kids if you make the trip to Illinois?"

Joe said, "Yes, but . . ."

I could tell that Joe was getting ready to tell me why he shouldn't have to make the extra effort and why it was unfair to him, and so on. In other words, Joe immediately got stuck on the rock called "but."

The word "but" is almost always a sign of resistance, one of the three core components always present in drama. In one of my favorite books, *Do It! Let's Get Off Our Buts*, the authors, John Rogers and Peter McWilliams say "but" means, "Behold the Underlying Truth" (Rogers and McWilliams 1991, 17).

I was correct about my perception. Joe continued, "But . . . I'm paying child support. I should not have to drive all the way to Illinois to see my kids."

By the way, "should" is also a word indicating resistance. Many people get stuck in the drama of what should or shouldn't be. Yes, you can fight that battle, if winning a battle is what you want. But again, in order to clear the fog and help Joe get clarity, I asked, "If there are two islands you can go to, and one means winning a battle with your wife and the other island is getting to see your kids and be a father to them—then which island would you choose?"

He said, "Seeing my kids, but . . ."

I said, "No buts. Are you willing to drive to Illinois several times a year and spend quality time with your kids, even if Patty does nothing more to cooperate?"

Joe said, "Yes."

(If I had an "Easy Button" this would be the time to press it!)

It's never as difficult as we make it when we get clear on what we can control and what we are committed to. I told Joe to keep this clarity and I could almost guarantee that his ex-wife would come around. However, even if she doesn't, he will still have been able to accomplish his goal of being in touch with his kids and maintaining that relationship, while advancing professionally in a career and location of his choosing.

The point here is that clarity may or may not change Joe's ex-wife. Joe will struggle if that is his motive or intention.

However, Joe's clarity will give him the essence of what he really wants, if he is able to let go of distractions and not get stuck on the rocks that lie between him and his final goal: being a good dad to his kids and advancing himself professionally in his new career. Do you see that while this kind of clarity may not change all the drama, it will give you peace and free up your energy for more productive endeavors?

Now I hope you see how personal drama spills over into your professional life and how clarity can change any situation. My question to you is this: As a leader, is there something you need to clear up in your personal life that is impacting your decision making, your ability to communicate, or your leadership style?

How Clarity Can Change Your Business

Several years ago I was working with Jane, a savvy business owner of a window-washing company. After a coaching session, we determined that she needed to increase her revenue by $5,000 per week, and that in order to do so, she needed her crew to complete $800 to $1,000 worth of work in eight hours and sell more services for the following week. The challenge was to have the work done without adding overtime and to keep selling more services with each completed job.

At first, Jane thought this was impossible and kept asking me how we could do this. I asked, "Why don't we trust that the 'how' will show up if we first make the commitment?"

Jane got her clarity, and then scheduled a meeting with her staff to talk about the new plan. At first, her team balked. "How is that possible?" they asked. They almost got stuck on the rock called *how*—but Jane reminded them that if they focused on the goal, the how would start revealing itself to them.

After just one meeting and within 24 hours, Jane was excited. The team booked $1,000 for the following two days and $700 more on the next day. Jane laid out a trial incentive plan, which further motivated the team. Once the leader got completely clear and communicated the expectations to her team, it was relatively easy to increase the revenues to $5,000 more per week.

HOW TO GAIN CLARITY

Earlier, we talked about how being stuck in the fog can cause a lot of confusion and a lack of alignment. The first step to clearing that fog is to gain clarity on your values and goals, as we discussed. Here are three questions you must answer in order to become clear on your objectives:

1. Who am I?
2. What do I want?
3. What am I committed to?

Spend time thinking about this, and put pen to paper. How you define yourself, what you say you want, and what you claim to be committed to will not only help clear the fog, it will also give you your "true north," so to speak. If you aren't sure about what you want, you now know what your next step is—to define it. Answering the "what am I committed to" question will clear a lot of fog. If you meditate on these three questions and think deeply about your life and business, you will come to know what behaviors to eliminate, where you are wasting time, and what exactly is draining your energy.

Your actions and words either align with what you have just said, or they point to significant problems. Either way, you have now gained awareness and cleared the fog.

I once held a position where I used to see myself as nothing more than a factory worker. My only commitments were to receive a paycheck and do the things in life that I enjoyed. The point of change came for me when—while still operating as a line worker in a factory—I decided that one day I would be a professional speaker, author, and trainer. This became my island.

By deciding to row in that direction, I cleared the fog. I wasn't there yet, but I knew where I was headed. Making that commitment allowed me to begin to change and become more efficient in my journey.

I have found that journaling can be a helpful way to get clear. In my journaling in those early years, I made a commitment to what I call "ICARE." ICARE stands for Improving Communication and Relationships Everywhere. That commitment prompted everything else to change. Because I was now dedicated to communication and relationships, I could no longer engage in petty disagreements and game-playing at work. I could no longer use sarcasm to make a point or roll my eyes when I disagreed. I had to change my behaviors—and these alterations came easily to me, because they were motivated by spiritual ideas and values-based principles, rather than a rule book.

If you don't know who you are and what principles you are committed to, then any wind will sway you. As I stated earlier, values matter. They shape your life and business.

Every business has a mission statement, and many have a vision statement as well. I would venture to guess, however, that most of these could not be repeated by most employees, because they get stuffed in a binder somewhere, rather than put on display as a means of inspiring people to move ahead. Zappos employees, however, can recite their core values. Let me give you a couple of examples: Zappos CEO Tony Hsieh says in his book, *Delivering Happiness: A Path to Profits, Passion, and Purpose*, that money is not enough to bring happiness. People want to work for passion, profits, and purpose. According to Hsieh, happiness consists of four things: "perceived progress, connectedness, perceived control, and being part of something bigger than self" (Hsieh 2010, 232). Two of Zappos's 10 core values are intriguing: *Create fun and a little weirdness,* and *pursue growth and learning.* To quote the Zappos web site, "We don't want to become one of those big companies that feels corporate and boring. We want to be able to laugh at ourselves. We look for both fun and humor in our daily work."

The Zappos finance department reportedly has a weekly parade called "random acts of kindness," where they select three employees at random, present them with a gift, put a hat on them, and take their picture.

The company's commitment to the core value of pursuing growth and learning led them to start a company library with books available to all staff and visitors.

These ideas and principles can be implemented on some level in even small businesses or private practices. The challenge is to build a mission for your life and your business that propels you forward and challenges you to stay the course—because you are either rowing to your island or you are not. You can either recite your mission or you can't. If you have to look it up, it's no good.

If you say that you are committed to teamwork but allow one team member to bully the others, then you are not really living your commitment. When you claim to be committed to open communication but keep skipping meetings with staff because you are too busy, you're not only stuck in the fog—you are also out of alignment. This occurs when you know what you want but aren't implementing actions to make it happen. You will eventually experience drama and endure something that I call the "integrity gap"—a concept that we'll discuss in detail in Chapter 2.

In a nutshell: If you want to be clear, you must know who you are, clearly state what you want, and define the values and principles to which you are committed. If you need a little help going deeper, spend quiet time considering the following questions. Your answers will tell you a lot.

Questions to Answer

1. What are my top 10 principle-based values?
2. What areas of my life or business are in the fog?
3. What are some of the distractions that take me off course?
4. Where do I get stuck?
5. Where can I improve as a leader?
6. What drama do I see on a daily basis in the workplace?
7. What drama do I see in my personal life?
8. Where am I avoiding or procrastinating?

Key Points

- One reason you don't have what you want is because you don't know what you want.
- Defining exactly what you want will increase clarity and lead you in the right direction.
- Drama is always due in part to a lack of clarity.
- The one with clarity navigates the ship.
- The words "but" and "should" are signs of resistance.
- The order of achieving your goals is figuring out "what," "who," and then "how."
- As a leader, your lack of clarity is creating more drama.
- Clarity can change any situation.
- Both peace and prosperity are equally important in eliminating drama from your life.

Chapter 2

Identify the Gap

People only see what they are prepared to see.
—Ralph Waldo Emerson

Besides a lack of clarity, the most likely reason that you're experiencing drama is that you get *stuck in the gap*—the place between where you were and where you want to be. If your goal stretches you even a little, it's important to keep in mind that your goal always looks easier to achieve than it is. Case in point: As a child, I was a very good swimmer. My family used to visit a lake each weekend, and every weekend I would beg my mother to let me swim to a nearby island. It looked so easy, and I was absolutely dying to try it.

My mother's answer, however, was always no. Even though I tried my best to persuade her that I could make it to the other side, she knew it wasn't nearly as easy as it looked to me. That decision in itself was an example of good leadership.

Sometimes you do what you know is best—even if those under you do not understand or agree.

As a leader, it takes wisdom and recognition to realize that no matter how accessible a goal seems it nearly always looks easier to achieve than it is. You don't always know what will be required up front, or the changes and obstacles that may occur along the way.

Whether you are initiating change or being forced to change because of the economy, outside threats, someone else's decisions, or new legislation, any significant adjustment throws you into that gap of the unknown. It's a place that's full of surprises where much is required of you. Very often, the power of newfound vision and clarity is so strong that it is tempting to jump into the boat with no map and only one oar.

There is most likely an instance in your life where you can recall being very excited about a goal—that is, until you got about halfway through. You were smack dab in the middle of the gap, and felt hopeless. Getting where you wanted to be was much more difficult than you had initially imagined. You hadn't realized what was going to be required of you to reach your goal; perhaps you thought it was going to take a lot less time or money. You compared your situation with that of someone else who had more experience and more resources. You, on the other hand, were out of resources and low on motivation—and the end was nowhere in sight.

Having worked for more than 14 years in human resources and as an organizational change consultant for Fortune 500 companies, certified coach Shawn Driscoll noticed that there are stages of change. Driscoll said in a personal interview with me that there is a momentous point on the way to reaching any significant goal where something that she refers to as a "valley of despair" takes place.

Driscoll explains, "We are looking at the goal and it looks farther than it ever did before. This is the risky stage where many of us retreat. In addition, this is where most of us say, 'If I had known what I know now, I would have never started.'"

Even small changes can create big drama. This phenomenon is as true for the individual as it is for a small business or large corporation. Identifying the gap is about giving yourself and your team the resources to weather the storm and withstand the drama in the gap. The saying I cited previously, "A stitch in time saves nine," holds absolutely true here. Prepare your team for the gap, and you will enjoy a successful journey.

The premise of the gap is:

1. The gap is the distance between point A and point B in reference to achievement.
2. The bigger the gap, the bigger the potential for drama.

If you lead a team of people, it is very important to identify the two types of gaps always present in change. It is equally vital to manage these gaps and communicate their existence to your team. Let's talk about the two kinds of gaps.

The First Gap: The Physical Journey

The first gap—the physical journey—involves all the practical ways you get from point A to point B. You plan, do a SWOT (Strengths, Weaknesses, Opportunities, and Threats) analysis, and hire the right team. You strategize, put together a marketing plan, and so on. You have undoubtedly heard many of these terms in your business training.

The Second Gap: The Nonphysical Journey

The second gap—the nonphysical journey—is something you might have heard less about. It is comprised of all the components of the spiritual, emotional, and mental processes you experience while getting from point A to point B.

My journey from factory worker to professional speaker, business owner, and author included the need for me to develop many practical and business skills, such as learning internet marketing, becoming proficient in writing and public speaking, hiring virtual assistants, finishing a master's degree, and learning foundational business skills. Although I had the vision and the desire, there was still a very large gap regarding practical skills and knowledge.

There was also another gap for which I was unprepared: the character-based, spiritual life lessons I had to learn in order to do the work I wanted. I didn't know about the pressure that would come with not having a regular schedule or a steady paycheck. I did not know things about the brain that I know now—that the brain craves certainty, or that when you feel threatened, all kinds of chemicals flush through your blood stream and make you feel even worse. I didn't know what kind of strength it would take to face rejection, listen to negative feedback, and compete for business even with good friends.

It is not easy to keep your attitude in check after losing a contract when you have worked very diligently to win the proposal. Many life lessons come as painful losses. I once made a mistake that cost me several thousand dollars.

The second gap is often the more challenging one. Even though you are operating on the nonphysical level, these nonphysical lessons eventually also manifest in the physical realm. These losses may teach you the importance of self-forgiveness, patience, and tenacity. You will see how these lessons are tied to practical business skills.

A professional speaker and author of *Discover True North: A 4-Week Approach to Ignite Your Passion and Activate Your Potential,* Anne Bruce talks about how the fear of success itself can occasionally prevent us from moving ahead. She writes, "Sometimes our greatest fear is not that we will prove to be inadequate or inferior, but that we will actually become more powerful, more intelligent, more perceptive, and more brilliant than we can now imagine. And if that happens, what next? How will your life change? How will all this affect the personal and professional relationships in your life? What will people think of you? Will people say 'Who do you think you are?' And will you care?" (Bruce 2004, 19).

As a leader, you must be aware of the psychological and physical changes your team undergoes when they are threatened with change. One way you lessen the drama is to identify the gap and develop a realistic view of your starting point—including your weaknesses and limitations individually, as a team, and even as a company. If you don't recognize any limitations and weaknesses before your journey begins, you are sure to see them along the way.

Any significant transformation will challenge you to overcome the drama in either the first or second gap. The sooner you accept this truth, the more fun you can have while navigating through the changes you are about to make.

How to Identify the Gap

Depending upon how complex your mission is, there are many ways to identify the gap. While you don't want to get lost in analysis paralysis, you can use these eight questions as a checklist:

1. What kind of tasks are necessary?
2. What kind of talent does your team need?
3. What is the financial investment required?
4. What are some potential problems you might face along the way?
5. Who or what has experienced something similar to your situation, so that you could ask for advice?
6. How long will it take?
7. What is required emotionally, mentally, and spiritually?
8. What is the exception wherein we say it's no longer worth it?

It is also good to know any statistics that can give you a success-to-failure rate in advance.

Shorten the Gap

My most pressing piece of advice in regard to how to address the gap is to intentionally "chunk it down." I also call this process *shortening the gap*—and it is a crucial part of any goal-setting process. Here's why: Even if it's possible for a leader or visionary to remain motivated during the difficult times, your team probably won't. You have to take care of those doing the rowing so that they stay engaged.

The founder of a successful motivational print company, Successories, and publishing company, Simple Truths, Mac Anderson, was quoted in *Attitude Digest* magazine: "When you set goals that are not realistic, your team is not motivated. If they have one doubt in their minds that they can reach that goal, then they are demotivated. But if it's realistic, they think they can do it, they are very motivated, and they move forward. Short term, one step at a time, just to get to the next plateau, and before you know it, you'll be a lot closer to the big dream that you started with" (Godfrey 2010, 41).

One of Mac's reportedly favorite quotes is, "Inch by inch, life's a cinch. Yard by yard, life is hard."

The visual I give is this: You see the big island and you are rowing toward it—but there are five small islands in between you and your final destination. Reaching each island is a cause for celebration. Your responsibility as a leader is to give the team a bigger purpose to row toward and create an experience of success. If you are always using the carrot and stick approach, you won't have a very cohesive team. People are naturally motivated when they are good at what they do, and also recognized for applying their skills in a way that aligns with their purpose while advancing the company. You have to make it possible for your team to succeed. There has to be an intrinsic reward in it for them, even if it is just the satisfaction of knowing that they reached a small stepping stone in the pursuit of a larger goal.

Get Real

Recognize as well that if you are making big changes that threaten your employees' security, then a meeting, a few pats on the back, and several stopping places along the way aren't going to help. Get real about this.

If you're going to eliminate people in the process of your change, you need to be honest. If people's job descriptions or responsibilities are going to change or increase, you must tell the truth; and you need to get their input instead of keeping it from them.

This has the potential to be a huge, jagged rock in the gap if this is going on. You must find a way to deal with this problem. If the people whom you want to help you are the ones about to lose their positions, acquire a doubled work load, or lose something while the company makes gains, it is not going to be pretty.

However, a measure of honesty can help them in the transition. You can refer them to other companies, or assist them in finding a different job. If you support them and respond to their needs, they will appreciate you and help you through the change more than they would have if you had thrown them a boomerang.

Find a way to make them want to help you. Be honest. Seek their ideas. Share in the financial rewards when possible. Anything that makes the experience more pleasant for your team members will certainly make it easier on you.

Implement a Trial Period, and Reassess the Gap

When I'm coaching or consulting a business owner about an impending change, I always suggest that they establish a trial period. I recommend that they set a few limitations or time to reassess in the midst of any change. This makes it much easier to adjust your course when something doesn't work out—and it definitely beats going back on your word. In reality, this is all about managing expectations and delivering more than you promised.

Consider how easy it is to promote a great employee to supervisor. That seems like a minor change, doesn't it? You have a good worker who has been with you for several years, has a great record, and knows all the systems—so you offer a promotion. Then, all of a sudden, the power goes to her head, and you see a whole other person emerge. This takes place because there is still a gap between this employee's experience being a "worker bee" and getting accustomed to leading others. The pressure is too great and now you've created a monster. You didn't think the other employees would be so jealous. Maybe there are things going on of which you are unaware. You aren't sure—but you wish you could take back the promotion and start over.

What happened here? In essence, there was a much bigger gap than you anticipated. You didn't realize that just because someone is a great worker, she may not have people skills or the emotional capacity to deal with the pressures of leadership. You may have underestimated your employee's level of maturity, or perhaps you failed to recognize the importance of training or the necessity of creating a system for advancement. There were no stopping places between worker bee and full-blown supervisor.

But what if you would have had a way to measure effectiveness for three months before giving the official promotion? This simple practice could have helped you identify a huge gap in your promotions system. This way, you would have not promised anything, and instead used the three months as a training ground for ideas or as a cross-training technique. You could have also created a list of criteria for the kind of skills and characteristics that must be in place before giving this kind of promotion. That approach would allow you to see how your team responds emotionally to someone else's leadership. In addition, this method can potentially help the employee save face in the event the person is not a good fit for the job. Since status is right at the top of many people's most fervent needs, you need to take the necessary precautions when altering someone's status.

Scheduled Communication

As I already stated, it is crucial to define the gap—and, once goals are set, to celebrate the small successes along the way. It is equally important to keep identifying the gap throughout the journey, adjusting as you go. You can easily complete all of these undertakings by holding a weekly meeting with your team.

I always get a lot of excuses and resistance when I suggest that people hold a weekly meeting. However, I promise that once you know how to use this tool effectively, you'll realize how it can eliminate a lot of mistakes, add to the team camaraderie, and improve morale.

The two biggest mistakes I see in weekly meeting implementation are that the leader does not know how to create an agenda and stick to it, and/or does not know how to promote engagement during the meeting. The meeting drags on, turns into a complaint session, or becomes yet another "let me tell you what you need to do" monologue.

Your agenda needs to have an allotted amount of time for ideas and feedback, as well as a period to recognize outstanding achievements and honor those who have shown exceptional character during difficult times. Making this commitment on a weekly or bimonthly schedule will help your team maintain excitement. Failing to do so will most likely elicit the problems associated with drama in the gap.

A few signs that there is drama in the gap:

- ◆ Your team is overworked and overwhelmed.
- ◆ There is never any cause to celebrate.
- ◆ There is never enough time, resources, or money.
- ◆ You witness a loss of motivation.
- ◆ Team drama and petty bickering break out due to stress.
- ◆ Loss of joy or loss of humor is prevalent.
- ◆ Finger-pointing is rampant.

Challenges in the Gap

Obviously, the problems in the gap are much like the problems that come when you're stuck in the fog. Here's why: You always lose clarity once you get stuck in the gap. Getting stuck in and of itself is an indicator that you have lost clarity. Remember—all drama has one thing in common: a lack of clarity. The clearer you are, the easier it is to stay the course and deal with the challenges in the gap. When you get out of alignment with your goal (the physical gap), or who you are (the nonphysical gap), this creates what I call the *integrity gap*: something that will reveal your innermost challenges of character and hidden agendas.

The Integrity Gap

One definition of integrity is to be "complete or undivided." When I hear the word integrity, I sometimes think of what happens when a computer is corrupted; it is out of integrity. The lack of integrity on a personal level suggests being double-minded, wishy-washy, and indecisive.

Let's say, for example, that you decide to have weekly meet-ings because you believe that they support your desire to engage the staff and keep everyone rowing in the same direction. Your new island is called "having weekly meetings." However, once you schedule the meeting, Mary—your star employee—throws a fit and starts complaining about how meetings are a waste of time. You feel conflicted; Mary is like your right hand. You truly want her support in any modifications that you make for your team. Now you have a competing island about 90 degrees to the left, called "making sure Mary agrees."

At this point, you are incomplete and divided. You have two desires that are not in alignment. You cannot simultaneously go to the island called "making Mary happy" and the island called "having weekly meetings." If you take the turn to the left even once, you end up off course. The integrity gap means that your choices are at odds with one another—a rift that clouds your clarity and pushes you off track.

You will always know there is an integrity gap when you feel confused. For example, I recently heard from a client about all the drama occurring in his workplace. He told me that he was unable to do his very best work because doing so would highlight the less-than-stellar job his supervisor was doing. He had all kinds of excuses as to why he could not confront the problem, why he could not offer his best to his company, and why he was stuck between a rock and a hard place.

It's important to realize that any instance in which a lower-status person must speak to their superior is registered by the brain as a threat. Ask yourself exactly where you are unclear any time you are stuck. Are there competing values at play—such as the importance of doing a good job versus the desire to protect your boss? What hidden intention is standing in your way and contributing to the gap?

My client had a hidden intention of avoiding conflict and protecting his boss, which he used as an excuse to steer clear of the confrontation and not do his best work. If he understood that in order to do his best work he must be willing to confront his challenges with his supervisor, he could have made a decision based on integrity. The decision to deal with the situation would have supported both the company's values and his own values of a strong work ethic. However, the decision to "play small" and try to slip under the radar in order to avoid confrontation would be out of alignment with supporting the organization's overall mission.

When your vision competes with one of your desires—and that desire is not in alignment with your direction—you're faced with an integrity gap that will divide you.

Anyone who has ever gone on a diet understands this principle. You want to look better and lose weight, but that ice cream sandwich is calling your name. It's easy to notice the integrity gap when the two desires are at opposite ends of the spectrum (the desire to look and feel better versus desire to consume something tasty).

You can't be committed to health and continue to smoke cigarettes; you can't be committed to being a good leader and want everyone to be your friend; you can't be committed to excellence and continue to yell at your employees; and you can't be committed to teamwork while making excuses about poor communication.

Competing desires always cause drama. I constantly see leaders dodge difficult conversations (sometimes with themselves) that would have saved them a lot of frustration. However, they have a hidden agenda of keeping the peace momentarily, making sure they don't offend the office drama queen, or avoiding the boring task of writing paperwork or filing a report. Though these reasons are perfectly understandable, they're not always helpful in the end.

If you are unaware of your divisions and distractions, you will eventually pay the consequences later.

Many times, our competing goals are out of our conscious awareness, and the lines become a bit blurred. For example, your goal of doubling your business competes with your goal of attending all of your child's ballet recitals. Or your intention of being liked competes with your desire to eliminate tardiness and increase productivity.

Every significant goal or vision you create will eventually test you in some way. In his book, *The Dip: A Little Book That Teaches You When to Quit (And When to Stick)*, author Seth Godin talks about the natural low point that's always present when we pursue lofty goals (Godin 2007, 17). A good example of getting stuck in the gap is the medical office that decides to go from manila folders to electronic record keeping. At first, it seems exciting. But when employees have to work overtime or change their work habits—or when drama arises because someone doesn't understand how the new system works—it's easy to want to retreat and revert.

Managing Expectations Is Key to Keeping Drama at Bay in the Gap

Knowing what to expect in advance and keeping the return on investment in mind makes the gap more tolerable. Most of us understand the concept of underpromise and overdeliver when it comes to customer service, but we forget that the rule also applies to our staff. Think of your employees or team members as your internal customers and it will be easy to underpromise and over-deliver as you strive for an ambitious goal. When your vision is compelling enough—and when you know what is required and can get everyone invested—you will be courageous enough to navigate through the changes, challenges, and storms.

Illusions in the Gap

As you move through the gap, your commitments will be challenged. Your leadership abilities will be tested in ways that you are incapable of imagining from where you currently sit in the boat. Not only are there tests and temptations, there are also many myths and illusions you must navigate past while in the gap. One of these myths is that salvation is on the island.

Even large companies and their leaders encounter regular challenges to keep their commitments and navigate through the gap. Remember SAS, the private software company discussed earlier? As the tech bubble soared in 2000, SAS CEO Jim

Goodnight faced a situation that could have ruined the culture that he and his team had worked so hard to create. Goodnight was receiving a lot of pressure to take SAS public. While he might have considered this the island of salvation—if his only concern was attaining wealth and fame—Goodnight instead refused to go public. As a *USA Today* article, "SAS Workers Won When Greed Lost," published April 21, 2004, stated: "He said no against a powerful tide of conventional wisdom when saying yes would've vaulted him near the top tier of wealth and fame. His two-thirds ownership of SAS—pronounced 'Sass'—would've placed him a notch below the likes of Microsoft's Bill Gates and Oracle's Larry Ellison" (Maney 2004, 9).

By saying no, Goodnight, 61, saved his company's culture—a way of life so envied it was featured in 2003 on *60 Minutes* and consistently lands SAS near the top of *Fortune*'s annual list of best places to work. Saying no also allowed SAS to be one of the few tech companies to prosper during the 2001–2003 tech downturn.

There was something equally as important to the CEO of SAS as making money: the commitment to putting employees first. People who work at SAS currently enjoy free healthcare at an onsite clinic, a fitness center, and even a piano in the break room, and they still make a lot of money while keeping that commitment. Going public might have changed everything. It could have put the power into shareholders' hands—people who might have been willing to sacrifice what had been created solely for the sake of making profits.

When you get excited and inspired by your big vision—whether it's getting the new technology, hiring the right business manager, or moving to another location—it's easy to become so focused on achieving the goal (getting to the island) that you start to believe that all your problems will be solved once you arrive there. But there is always more to be achieved once you get to the island—and it's easy for disappointment to set in.

As a result, *the* drama becomes *your* drama. Instead of rowing together, the teams are beating each other with the oars—and negativity and complaining abound. *This is harder than I thought it would be. It's not fair. That's not my job.* We cling to the belief that once we get to the island everything will be back to normal.

The unfortunate truth, however, is that it's a lie. Drama in the boat does not equal paradise on the island. Drama in the boat, if not overcome, is almost a guarantee of more drama on the island.

Life Is Lived in the Gap

The fact is, life is always lived in the gap. You only visit the island. To that end, a COO once asked me, "If life is lived in the gap, why should we ever even try to get to the island?"

Here's why: Once you get to the island, you get to celebrate the accomplishments and completion of a worthy goal; in fact, that's why you need to shorten the gaps and have the regularly scheduled communication. Heck, you might get to stay on the island for a couple of months, or even several years. But eventually, the coconut juice doesn't taste as good as it once did, and your hammock gets a hole in it.

Because of the mere fact that you've landed on the island, your vision has expanded. You never knew there was yet another island 5,000 miles away. Now that you have experience in the gap, the gap actually beckons you to get out there again where life happens.

It is important to understand that salvation is never on the island, so get rid of language like "When X happens, then I'll be satisfied." Or, "When we make X amount of revenues, then we can celebrate and be happy." Be happy now, and start enjoying the journey. If you and your team can handle the drama in the gap, I guarantee it's going to be some amazing island celebration.

The Two Questions in the Gap

There are really only two questions you need to ask yourself to understand how to close the gap: Do I know what is required? Am I willing to do what is required?

I believe that life will test every commitment you make. I also believe it is very important to keep your commitments so that you learn to have a high level of trust for yourself. Every time you break a promise—to either yourself or someone else—you lose a little self respect, which impacts your ability to lead and take risks. To quote Stephen M. R. Covey, author of *The Speed of Trust*, "The foundation of trust is your own credibility, and it can be a real differentiator for any leader. A person's reputation is a direct reflection of their credibility, and it precedes them in any interactions or negotiations they might have. When a leader's credibility and reputation are high, it enables them to establish trust fast—speed goes up, cost goes down."

Developing yourself to be a trustworthy leader is an investment in your personal character, to help you lead with no regrets. I love the following quote from the late Jim Rohn: "We must all suffer one of two things: the *pain of discipline* or the *pain of regret*. The difference is discipline weighs ounces and regret weighs tons."

Think about politicians or leaders who seem to be overtly committed to promoting a cause. Only later, we find out that rather than contributing to this cause, they had become tempted off track, and had instead worked toward something that actually opposed the cause. When the news of their inconsistency became public, they no longer held any power to promote their purpose.

Regret is a heavy price to pay for a lack of discipline. It's thus important that we determine what potential tests and threats exist in the gap.

Passing the Gap Test

I want to share an example of how your vision, your commitment and passing the Gap Test all come into play. In 2003, Zappos CEO Tony Hsieh and his partner Fred Mossler made a new commitment to build the Zappos brand around customer service, and to apply the same goal toward the vendors, treating them as partners—a move which was unheard of in the industry.

A clear vision is just the beginning. Once the vision has been declared, the gap question is, "What is required of us?" So often as leaders, we say we are committed to something but fail to recognize that any bold commitment means there will be massive changes and sacrifice in order to close the gap. Once you gain clarity about the new island you want your team to row to, you are under the microscope and your actions either show your commitment or show your inconsistencies. This is as true for a company of 10 employees as it is for a Fortune 500 company.

What would be required for Zappos to build a brand of customer service was to give up easy money—in fact, 25 percent of their overall sales—by eliminating the drop shipping part of their business.

Even though drop shipping was easy money because it required no inventory and low risk, the problems with drop shipping were all related to customer service. Five percent of all drop-shipped orders were not able to be fulfilled, and the other 95 percent of orders were filled slowly, which translated to unhappy customers. Although the vision was in place, the action was not. "We did a lot of talking but we weren't putting our money where our mouths were, and our employees knew it," writes Hsieh in his book, *Delivering Happiness* (2010, 123).

Now you can see the integrity gap at play. On the one hand, there is the desire to make more sales through easy money, but doing so means sacrificing an even bigger vision of being the leader in customer service. In addition, the longer Zappos continued to talk about customer service but did not live up to the vision, the more the trust would erode inside the workplace.

"The longer we waited to pull the trigger, the more our employees would lose faith in us. In March 2003, with the flip of a switch we turned off that part of our business, and removed all drop ship products from our web site," Hsieh writes (2010, 124).

I encourage you to pick up a copy of Hsieh's book and read the rest of the details. Hsieh says this was both the easiest and hardest decision he had ever made.

Commitment	Requirement	Test
To build the Zappos brand around customer service.	Pay vendors on time and treat them like partners.	Dip in revenues.
	Eliminate drop shipping.	Cash flow problems.

Figure 2.1   Tony Hsieh's Gap Test

There is a simple test I use to initially identify the gap. I draw a diagram with three columns. On the first column, I write the word *commitment*. On the second, I write *requirements*. On the third, I write *test*.

Completing this "gap test" will help you to clarify any exceptions to your commitment, and be kind to yourself as you prepare for your journey. It also helps you define what you want out of your goal. By our choices, we reveal our commitments, and a real commitment will always be tested. If you want to see if you are willing to be committed to your vision, use the gap test. See how Hsieh's example is used in Figure 2.1.

The test in the gap, the third column, is where you try to predict any future events that might challenge you to keep your commitment. Any commitment, personally or professionally, will require you to take risks, make sacrifices, and navigate through change. As a leader, you will be tested in the first gap of making appropriate business decisions and leading your team. You will also be tested in the second gap, that nonphysical, spiritual place where you must align with your beliefs and the values that show your level of integrity and commitment even in difficult times. As Hsieh said in his book, your employees know when you are not walking your talk (2010, 123). Even more important, you know when you are not walking your talk. Walking your talk always stretches you and requires you to give up that which no longer serves your higher vision.

When I made a commitment to improving communication and relationships, it required me to change some bad habits. I have a very quick tongue and sharp wit. This always came in handy if I wanted to put people in their place, win an argument, or embarrass someone who had done me wrong. When I created a new vision, however, this created a gap between who I was and who I wanted to be. It was crystal clear what I needed to do. Later on, as I became a more competent communicator, I started to understand that changing any habit is not an overnight task. Understanding the tests helps you to stay focused and out of the fog.

How to fix problems in the gap:

- Have a measurement system and keep your team posted on progress.
- Keep revisiting the vision so that it remains clear.
- Shorten the big gap by establishing small benchmarks along the way.
- Rest and celebrate in between the gaps.
- Give your team the training and resources to help them.
- Reward and acknowledge success.
- Use weekly scheduled meetings to celebrate and update.

Questions to Answer

1. Do I know what is required to get from A to B?
2. Am I willing to do what is required?
3. Do we have a way to measure success?
4. Are there appropriate stopping places along the way?
5. What events or obstacles might test our commitment?

Learning Points

- The gap is the distance between where you are and where you want to be.
- There are two gaps: the physical and nonphysical.
- The second gap is the distance between who you are and who you want to be.
- There is always drama in the gap.
- The gap test helps you know what your challenges will be.

Chapter 3

Tell Yourself the Truth

Get your facts first,
then you can distort them as you please.
—Mark Twain

Whenever there is drama, there is usually a story operating somewhere. It doesn't matter if the drama is just in your own head, or if an employee is tattling on someone who looked at her the wrong way. Whatever the case may be—there is a story attached to it. But don't blame yourself or your team; as it turns out, we human beings are inherently built to tell stories.

Norman Farb, a scientist at the University of Toronto—and six of his colleagues—discovered in 2007 that human beings have distinct ways of experiencing their lives. The primary method is called *narrative circuitry*. The second way is *direct experience* (Rock 2009). Direct experience is what we might define as being present "in the now." This is something that can take a lot of effort, as evidenced by the number of books now written on the importance of experiencing "what is" as a way to release the mind chatter.

In contrast, the first way—narrative circuitry—takes in the information moment by moment, then filters it through your interpretations. In other words, we are all "meaning-making machines." Most of the time, we humans live life from the narrative circuitry point of view; and for the purpose of this book I refer to this way of experiencing our existence as "the story."

I define the story as the meaning we create from our life experiences. While it can be one version of the truth, it's also often comprised of half-truths, beliefs, assumptions, misjudgments—and some of the 60,000-plus thoughts entering our minds on any given day. In simple terms, our stories are our own interpretations about our lives that may or may not serve us. Most of

61

our way of understanding the world is simply something we make up that has been generated from our memories, upbringing, and filters that have been programmed into our brains since birth.

In the book *Buddha's Brain: The Practical Neuroscience of Happiness, Love, and Wisdom*, authors Rick Hanson and Richard Mendius make the claim that, "Much of what you see out there is actually manufactured in here by your brain, painted in like computer-generated graphics in a movie. Your brain simulates your world—each of us live in a virtual reality that is close enough to the real thing so that we don't bump into the furniture" (Hanson and Mendius 2009, 43).

I have studied how the brain works as well. I learned about the conscious and subconscious mind, and have interviewed top experts in the field who can tell you why humans do what they do. In a nutshell, your unconscious mind controls much of your life. You have programmed habits that run on autopilot. That is why there are so many versions of the truth and so many misunderstandings, hurt feelings, and drama. Although our stories protect us—by helping us avoid distasteful information—they can also hamper productivity.

You might be wondering—if our stories are based upon the unconscious, how is it possible to tell yourself the truth? That is a good question—and one that I will attempt to answer in part in this chapter. Let's first look at three premises of *Tell Yourself the Truth*.

The premises of *Tell Yourself the Truth*:

1. Everyone lives their lives from the stories they believe.
2. Your truth is only one version of a larger reality.
3. Denial is a way to avoid responsibility.

Why This Is Important

As a leader, you will waste a considerable amount of your time trying to dissect the stories and various shades of reality you hear. If you are not careful, you will get absolutely no work done because you will be putting out fires and finding yourself stuck in the middle—or even the scapegoat for some employee drama, customer service drama, or combination thereof.

Consider Valerie's experience. Valerie was called into her supervisor's office because of complaints from other employees. The supervisor informed Valerie that her colleagues had been complaining about her work and attitude, calling her a troublemaker and an instigator. Instead of feeling motivated and ready to facilitate positive change, Valerie's self-esteem was crushed along with any sense of belonging she had in her department. The supervisor made the mistake of only seeing one version of the truth, instead of looking for a more accurate sense of reality. Upon further investigation, the supervisor realized that because Valerie had transferred from another department, she had more seniority and expertise than the other workers. Her transfer meant that at least two people would be moved out of the department, and that she was in line for a possible promotion. Valerie admitted that while she was known for her sarcastic wit, other workers often encouraged it. Valerie thought she was just enjoying the camaraderie, and was clueless to the fact that she was being set up to look like the troublemaker. The true case was that the other workers felt threatened by her presence.

No matter what you think the truth is, there is always another, bigger reality. Listen for the red flags in the stories your staff tells you: the excuses about why things cannot change, why things just are the way they are, and how someone is doing someone wrong.

None of these excuses add one iota to problem solving or moving forward—and chances are that a big portion of what you hear is just the story. People resist looking at the bigger reality. We all trust our version of the truth; in fact, most of us initially defend our bad behavior whenever we're asked to change.

Justification Keeps You Stuck

Have you ever noticed that when you ask someone to change their behavior—be it sarcasm, eye-rolling, angry outbursts, or stubborn attitude—they will usually respond with something like "Oh, that's just the way I am"? Justification is one way that people regularly avoid taking personal responsibility. We make excuses for our behavior based on a litany of reasons—personality theory, horoscope, and the way we were raised.

I'm an ISFJ, or I'm a green; so that's why I always . . . blah blah blah.

I'm a Leo; therefore, I like to be in charge.

My numerology chart says I love freedom, so it's difficult for me to follow.

Have you noticed that no matter what you want to believe, you can always find some method that makes sense to you to back it up?

A better way to approach these self-awareness tools is to use them to better understand your strengths and weaknesses as a way to make positive change—not to make excuses for bad behavior or irresponsible patterns. One of the best systems of self-discovery and personal development is the "enneagram," a personality assessment based on nine distinct patterns of thinking, acting, and feeling that determine the nine major personality types. Dr. David Daniels, author of *The Essential Enneagram: The Definitive Personality Test and Self-Discovery Guide*, explained in one of my Attitude Builders audio programs, "Every human being has three basic needs, the need for security, the need for relationship, and the need for getting what we want. We try to get these needs met in different ways depending upon our personality type. Sometimes our ways work for us in a leadership capacity and sometimes our methods work against us." Dr. Daniels elaborated, "If we want to expand into self-mastery there is a universal growth process [which he calls] the 4 As: Awareness, Acceptance, Action, and Adherence. You can own your personality instead of letting it own you. Once you own your personality then you are liberated."

Imagine how liberating a workplace could be if each individual took charge of his responses in a team capacity—without being held captive by dysfunctional thought patterns, actions, and truths that do not serve him.

I challenge you to look differently at what you consider to be the truth about who you are—and I encourage you to consider that no matter what your astrological sign, personality type, life history, or habits, you still have choices, and the ability to influence change.

> **The following are some telltale signs that indicate errors in truth:**
>
> ◆ Frequent blowups.
> ◆ Walking on eggshells.
> ◆ Fear about a difficult conversation.
> ◆ Claiming that "I already know what he/she will say."
> ◆ Making decisions based on assumptions rather than facts.
> ◆ Hiding information.
> ◆ Receiving constant surprises and disappointment.
> ◆ Refusing to look at data and facts.
> ◆ Letting the bully get by with bad behavior.
> ◆ Engaging in hearsay, gossip, and exaggerations.
> ◆ Assuming you know someone else's intentions.

We all live our lives from our own personal truths. What do you believe to be true about your business, the economy, your team, or yourself? Do you believe leadership is difficult? Do you believe it is hard to find good employees? Are you living out these truths? What if you could change some of the things you previously thought to be true?

We've already discussed how our justifications keep us stuck in the story. Assumptions and white lies are a couple of other ways we create little stories to hold onto.

Assumptions

It is amazing to recognize all the assumptions from which we operate. I listen for the assumptions in my coaching; if I can spot them, I can facilitate the breakthrough. For example, I spoke with a client who complained that his crew showed up late for a bid. He threw a fit and went on to tell me how he was sick and tired of picking up their messes, and how they never took responsibility for their actions. After a bit of discussion, I discovered that this man had never even bothered to ask his crew why they were late. He made an assumption that they were simply shirking their duties, when in reality they were handling a client complaint— and even made another sale in the process. They were being responsible, but the boss made an assumption.

What are some of the many assumptions we make on a daily basis? Well, for example—when you hire someone, you assume you have made a good choice. You imagine that the new worker will be dependable, honest, trustworthy, and have the skills you need to help you accomplish your goals. You also assume that the person you just hired will have your best interests at heart.

However, many times, you find yourself disappointed by your assumptions. You didn't realize that this new employee has a bad habit of being late. You assumed that because he was so convincing about his skills, he would be great at sales. Instead, the best sales job the new salesperson ever gave was the one to get you to hire him.

What if you would have asked a few more questions? What if, in your hiring process, you had given your recruiter some character-based questions to test his thinking?

You can avoid assumptions by developing a habit of asking questions, and coming from a place of curiosity instead of blame. Todd Kashdan—a clinical psychologist, professor at George Mason University, and author of the book *Curious?: Discover the Missing Ingredient to a Fulfilling Life*—states that curiosity isn't about "whether we pay attention, but how we pay attention to what is happening" (Kashdan 2009). His book goes on to talk about how remaining curious can actually help us attain a higher level of fulfillment.

Self-Judgment and White Lies

If you learn to listen closely, you will catch yourself and others in self-judgment and white lies all too frequently.

I'm not very smart.

I would, but I don't have the time.

No, I'm not angry at all.

I already know how she will respond.

I don't really care about (money, health, love, what others think).

How the Story Keeps You Stuck

All of us create stories to help us make sense of the world. These stories then become the beliefs and personal truths from which we live our lives.

I can't tell you how many times I have been coaching a manager who needed to go talk to the boss about some big employee issue. I would always hear some version of a story such as "I already know what he will say," or "He will never listen to anything negative about his star employee."

Really? Is that the truth—or do you just not know how to make a business case for this relationship issue? What if you had proof to back up the fact that you lost $20,000 last year due to the star employee's behaviors?

"I already know what he will say" is a story that's very commonly told by someone in a lower position to avoid confronting someone in a higher position of power. It's a way to avoid responsibility and to protect one's self from an unpleasant conversation. If you already have assumptions in place, you've left no room for another truth to emerge.

Why It's Hard to Separate Story from Truth

There is always a kernel of truth in every story. Your past experience provides evidence of what you believe to be true.

In other words, you bring your past encounters and your filters about life into every present interaction.

For instance, you can recall the evidence of many times when your boss said exactly what you expected; therefore, you've mentally eliminated any possibility that he will ever respond differently. So, in order to make life easy, you simply create a story that removes any need to confront, ask for something different, or risk disapproval by standing your ground. Besides that, it feels good to be right about how things are.

Your Story Helps You Be Right and Avoid Responsibility

I believe once basic needs are met, every human being's most pressing desire is to be right—even if being right is not in your best interest.

I met a homeless man once while in Chicago in the middle of December. He was freezing cold and lived in the alley right behind where I was standing to wait for my cab to the airport. He asked me if I had a hat. I had a scarf, but I didn't want to give it to him; so I told him I would give him money to go get a hat. But it wasn't really so much about the hat. He had a story that he wanted me to hear.

He told me he had been arrested for murder. After I jumped a foot off of the ground, he said "Don't worry . . . I didn't really do it"—so I gained my composure and listened intently. He was never convicted, but he did spend time in jail and was now without a job. I asked him why he didn't at least try to get some money to get back on his feet.

He replied, "No one will hire me."

I said, "Well, here you are living in this alley here by this hotel. What if you just asked if you could wash dishes or take out trash? Just something to help you regain some of your power and give you some hope—not to mention a little money to prove you can make the shift? Have you even tried to ask?"

He told me he hadn't. Since the possibility did not even exist in his mind, it could therefore not occur in his life. He wasn't even willing to entertain the "what if" of it all—because his previous experience and assumptions kept him from giving himself even a fighting chance.

This man was in a state of shame; he already had an ending to his story. He was too afraid of rejection to try. He already knew the answer.

The point here is not about who is right—it is that he gets to be right without taking the risk of proving it.

Stories are designed to keep you safe and to prove that you are right—to make you feel like there is nothing else you can do. Stories help you avoid responsibility and the risk of rejection. They let you justify the reasons why things are the way they are.

The problem with stories is they take away your power of choice and eliminate your sense of awareness. This is called *denial*.

Denial: The Drug of Choice

If you are in a position that requires you to bring awareness to someone of a higher rank than you—perhaps your boss or a business owner—it's likely going to be an uphill battle if you're engaging in denial. For example, let's say that you manage a private practice for a doctor. Even though the doctor is the boss, you are the cocaptain. You see things the doctor does not see; but you hate to tell the doc that his star nurse is a bully.

In other words, someone in your boat is beating everyone else with the oars. Of course no one else is rowing—because they're made to feel like they can never get it right. If the bully was gone, your little boat would go faster because everyone would be rowing in the same direction. Unfortunately, the captain thinks that if the bully goes, so does the business.

But you know differently. If you speak up, you may be thrown overboard; so you stay quiet and go down to the boiler room to shovel coal instead of taking your position on the top deck.

It's your job to navigate, to take care of people issues, and help create a profitable practice. And that's why you avoid the difficult conversation. You think that you already know what the doctor will say, so you don't risk putting yourself in a troublesome position. It's also why you keep trying to avoid the difficult conversation you know you need to have.

In short, you choose denial so you don't have to face the pain.

I describe denial in my workshops as though it were like a drug. If, for example, you were to have open-heart surgery, you would take an anesthetic to keep you from feeling any pain. This drug would enable the surgeon to go in and do his work. However, in order to recover, you must slowly come off the drug—which can be a very painful process. You would need a fair amount of tender loving care and support as you regained your health.

Coming out of denial is like coming off a drug.

Think back to a time when you have had to give a less than positive review to someone in a lesser position than you—perhaps an employee of yours. How did it feel? Or, perhaps you can remember a time when someone told you something about yourself that you didn't want to face. You might even beat yourself up for having such a big ego when you resist getting feedback—but remember to be gentle with yourself. One of the difficult scenarios for your brain is when your status feels threatened, and hearing what you don't want to hear takes you down a notch. It's no wonder that most of us prefer denial to degradation.

Authentic conversations can be somewhat painful. Some people are more mature about handling unwanted information than others, and your status on the totem pole has a large part to play in the dynamics of this. If you work for a control freak, egomaniac, or know-it-all, you must deliver unhappy news with skill and a high level of consciousness. On the other hand, there's not as much drama to deal with if you're communicating with a recently hired employee. She is new, you are in a much higher position, and there's not much history or much of a status threat.

If, however, you need to visit a touchy subject with the one with the most seniority, who is stubborn, and comes from the mantra of "that's the way I've always done it," it's going to be a little messier. If there is some scary truth you need to face or share with someone, it's going to require some courage, support, and conscious communication skills so you are both strong enough to recover, no matter what your position, or level of authority.

If you understand how denial works, you can be supportive and courageous at the same time. You can be a witness to the employee's pain without getting sucked into her drama. You also can open the field of possibility for her instead of coming from an assumption that she cannot handle the new truth or that she cannot change.

Communicating Upward with One in Denial

What is the best way to communicate with someone who is in denial—specifically, when she is in a position equal to yours or in a leadership capacity over you? I call this skill "owning your stuff." Start with the safest path—your part of the problem. Let's return to the example of running a private practice physician's office. Everything is great, except for the fact that one doctor, let's call him Dr. Headinsand, keeps overriding your decisions because his favorite nurse comes to him begging for special favors. Because Nurse Getmyway was his first support system at the office, he feels an obligation to keep her happy no matter what. Pleasing her is his natural default—and the end result is a lack of consistency. Many of the other staff are getting upset with his favoritism, and you are losing control.

Your first step is to request a 15-minute appointment with the doctor before office hours. You want to make sure he is fresh and not stressed, and informed that you have some important information that is impacting the practice. This alerts him that what you have to say is important enough to merit a special meeting.

In addition, this approach will not take him off guard. When you get together in your meeting, you tell him that you have something to confess and you need to apologize. Now he can let his defenses down, and doesn't have to worry about being threatened. I'm going to share a method with you that's part of a communication workshop I teach called The LABOR Principles. LABOR stands for Listen, Ask for What You Want, Boundaries, Own Your Stuff, and Represent Yourself. As I mentioned previously, this is the "O" part: Own Your Stuff. The first thing you have to do here is to own the part of the problem that is yours. This allows the other person go to a safe place where he can listen without feeling vulnerable.

Your discussion would go something like this. "Dr. Head-insand, I have a confession to make. I have been keeping something from you that has been bothering me. I know my job is to make this practice the best it can be, but I haven't told you about this because I didn't want to be a nuisance to you. Now I realize that it was not at all fair to you to be kept in the dark about something that is negatively impacting your practice. So, here it is.

"I need to know if you are willing to back me up when I make a policy—even if it becomes uncomfortable for you. My questions pertain to how Head Nurse Janelle Getmyway always requests that you change the rules or procedures of projects I've been working on. This has impacted our practice by [this is where you cite specific dollar amounts lost, employee negativity, absenteeism, or anything else that lets the doctor know you are serious about this problem]. I am sorry for hiding this from you, but I have to admit I was nervous asking for support."

The next step is to be specific about what you need him to do. "I need you to tell Janelle that these decisions are left to the administrator, and that we three will have to have a meeting if she is having problems with the leadership." Then you ask a magical question, "Are you willing to do that the next time Janelle or any of the staff come to you with a complaint?"

You will want to follow up by discussing a policy change at the next team meeting—and you want the doctor to be there backing you up. Let the team know that you are in charge of major decisions, and that anyone who approached the doctor with a request to override you is out of due process. He or she will be held accountable by some disciplinary action, which you will then explain in very factual language with no emotion and no drama. Explain that you are employing this tactic because it keeps everyone on the same page.

The point in this example is that a doctor should not be dealing with drama. He should be taking care of patients in need; that is why there is an administrator. This particular scenario is a prime example of a lack of clarity on who is in charge, the mission and purpose, as well as an example of how denial and secret-keeping create drama.

How to Facilitate Change

There are four things you need to do to facilitate change:

1. Become more aware of what is going on around you.
2. Create a conscious habit.
3. Step into a new truth.
4. Course-correct.

First, you have to develop a better sense of awareness. When you become more aware, you can learn how to separate fact from fiction.

For example—become aware of the lies that you tell yourself about people's inability to change. The popular belief in the past was that people were hardwired, that they were the way they were and couldn't do much to change. However, more recent scientific research offers good news: We can change. We are not hardwired. Our brains actually have some degree of plasticity. How great!

According to neuropsychologist Rick Hanson, as stated in one of my Attitude Builders monthly teleseminar programs,

"The truth is that the brain is particularly susceptible to change in the first year or two of life, but keeps changing over the life-span—and with the power of self-directed neuroplasticity, anyone can use their mind to change their brain to change their life!"

The bad news is that in order to change, you first have to become aware that you may be making it all up. Most of us find it very difficult to admit that we might have been wrong all along about our views of life and others. As I mentioned previously, the need to be right comes right after our need for basic necessities like air, food, and water.

Create New Habits

Once you are willing to see the potential error of your ways, you must be prepared as well to create new habits—a process that takes place through the conscious mind.

There are four levels of consciousness, as taught in academia:

Level 1=Unconscious incompetence

Level 2=Conscious incompetence

Level 3=Conscious competence

Level 4=Unconscious competence

Remember what it was like when you started driving? You were nervous. You had to concentrate. You couldn't multitask. You had to remain conscious and remind yourself to make every move. You probably started out at Level 2, conscious incompetence. You weren't very good at it, but at least you knew it. Then as you practiced, it became easier and easier; however you still had to think about it a little bit. You then reached Level 3, conscious competence. Then one day, you could drive, change the radio, and talk on your cell while backing out of your driveway. In other words, you eventually did it without having to consciously think about it. (Not that I recommend these driving behaviors!)

Repeating and practicing unhealthy behaviors causes them to become ingrained in your life in the same way. Bad habits always come back to bite you. If you do something long enough, it becomes automatic. In other words, you eventually operate from the unconscious programming built in by habit.

The point is that you can reprogram yourself for success. You do this through heightening awareness, then intentionally creating new habits.

Why is this important to you personally? Because if you want to change results, you have to step into a new truth.

Stepping into a New Truth

You can encourage yourself and your staff to step into a new truth. This means that you will develop new habits that serve as evidence of a different truth. Of course, this brings us back to square one and square two: You must get clear about the new truth, then identify the gap. (See how this system works?)

What new truth do you need to tell yourself? All you have to do is rid yourself of denial, comprehend the new truth, and then look for evidence to support it.

Let me give you a personal example of a new truth I had to create. Like many people, I used to be reluctant to ask for what I really wanted. I had been taught not to ask for things when I was a child. I learned that any time I got what I wanted, someone had to sacrifice their needs so that mine could be met. When I did receive something I had been wanting, I was told about the sacrifices that were made so that I could be happy. I always felt a little guilty every time I got something I wanted; therefore, it did not feel good to ask for and have my desires met. These experiences led me to develop stories about money, value, and self-worth.

This outlook eventually influenced the way I viewed my value in business. Instead of seeing money as a way of trading value for value, my views of money put me in a no-win truth. I placed too high a value on money and the things it could buy, because I believed in sacrifice and scarcity more than I believed in value for value. To that end, I found it difficult to charge for my services; I truly thought that those who wanted and needed my services could not afford them, or that they had to sacrifice too much to trade their money for what I had to offer (as my parents had done in buying me things I wanted).

It's not difficult to figure out how this story impacted me on both a personal and professional level. When I finally came out of denial, I had to step into a new truth by changing my belief system. I created a belief that "my clients are resourceful and they make good decisions with their money." Then, instead of feeling guilty for my pricing, or obligated to work at no charge, I gave the responsibility to the clients to decide what was right for them. This helped me to offer my services at the right price and not to take it personally if it was not a good fit at the time. Every time I made a sale, I then wrote it down as evidence of a new truth.

This doesn't mean, however, that once you step into a new truth, the old truth doesn't sometimes emerge. You will go backward from time to time—which is why you must course-correct.

Course-Correct

It takes a while for new habits to become your truth. In other words, you will not be unconsciously competent at a new habit for quite some time. You may see an old pattern pop up even one year later, after you thought you had changed a habit for good. That is why it is vital to course-correct along the way.

For example, let's say that you want to get out of the habit of speaking and thinking negatively. There will be times when you may have to catch yourself, apologize, and rephrase your statement. Holding yourself accountable will add just enough pain that you won't want to backslide again.

How to Separate Fact from Fiction—The Grid:
A Tool for Dissecting the Story

I developed the Grid as a tool to help managers and leaders dissect the story from the facts. It's too easy to get caught up in who did what and who is to blame. In order to get to the heart of the matter, it is important to know the difference between fact, thought, and feeling. All stories are created from the combination of thought and feeling—not from fact. Knowing your feelings does not change the facts, but knowing the facts can change your feelings.

Let's imagine a scenario in which your colleague Melissa is working on a conference. While making arrangements, she discovers what she believes to be a mistake: The room that was reserved is way too small. Melissa's first reaction is disgust. She delegated the room reservation to Judy, whom she directly supervises. She calls you to discuss the situation and get another manager's advice before going to her boss to blow the whistle.

"I'm furious. I asked Judy to take care of getting the conference room for the party, and what does she do? She gets a small room for 200 people. The client is going to be furious. I knew I couldn't trust anyone else with these details."

As a fellow manager, what would you advise Melissa? Should she fire Judy? Do you both agree that your employees are incompetent? Should she just cover for Judy so the big boss doesn't see the drama? See Figure 3.1.

The story is always created between thought and feeling. Suppose we learn how to dissect the information. We might look for the facts and realize that only 10 people are going to meet in

Fact	Thought	Feeling
The room is 12 × 18.	The room is too small.	Upset
	The client will think I'm incompetent.	Anger
	It is Judy's fault for not reserving in advance.	Frustration

Figure 3.1   The Grid Tool

the room, or we might discover it's simply a communication glitch. Maybe there's a new meeting planner who didn't realize two partitions could be taken out to expand the room. Perhaps the boss meddled in the affair and asked Judy directly to get another room for a preconference VIP event.

As you can see, there are many things we might discover when we look at the facts.

The two questions you can ask are:

1. What are the facts?
2. What is the story?

As you can see, truth as we each define it is very subjective. Don't go on a mission to search endlessly for the ultimate truth in each story you hear; doing so will only enhance the drama. Your main objective should be to get to the desired outcome, and prevent future glitches by discerning what caused the glitch in the first place.

Instead of jumping to conclusions, or looking for who is at fault, realize that there are many stories which are all part of a bigger reality. Simply understand that all of us operate from programming within the subconscious mind. Our stories are made up of thoughts, feelings, and assumptions, mixed in with a few facts. Emotions have their place—even in the business world (we talk more about this in later chapters). In a nutshell, knowing how to discern fact from fiction efficiently is good leadership. But what happens when you have to correct others by sharing an uncomfortable "truth" with them? In their book *The Power of Full Engagement: Managing Energy, Not Time, Is the Key to High Performance and Personal Renewal,* authors Jim Loehr and Tony Schwartz remind us that there is always an optimal value at which anything becomes toxic, and that truth must often be delivered cautiously and in small doses. Too big of a dose can be overwhelming and self-defeating. To quote: "If the truth is to set us free, facing it cannot be a onetime event; rather it must be a practice" (Loehr and Schwartz 2003, 163). Telling the truth to both yourself and others must become a part of who you are as a leader, if you want to lead from integrity. Being honest with yourself involves your willingness to see beyond the stories to recognize the facts, and making decisions based upon those facts.

Once you understand the concepts in this chapter, they will help you diffuse arguments, make better business decisions, and even make better choices about hiring, firing, and promoting. Mastering these principles will show you areas in your own life that keep you stuck in your own story. If you are a leader, the faster you get the truth, the quicker you can solve the problem that keeps you stuck.

Questions to Answer

1. What are the facts?
2. What are the thoughts and feelings?
3. What new habits need to be developed?
4. Where do we need to course-correct?

Learning Points

1. Much of what you believe to be true is actually someone else's fiction.
2. Assumptions and white lies contribute to drama.
3. The brain has plasticity; therefore, anyone can change.
4. Leaders must learn how to separate fact from fiction.
5. Avoiding the truth is a means of avoiding responsibility.
6. Coming out of denial can be painful.
7. The story is always created by thought and feeling.
8. You can create a new reality by creating new habits.

Chapter 4

Reinvent and Realign

Being powerful is like being a lady. If you have to tell people you are, you aren't.
—Margaret Thatcher

No matter what your official title or level within the organization, you have some idea of who you think you are—and that notion influences your leadership style. Who you think you are determines how you lead, respond to disappointment, deal with unfortunate circumstances, communicate, discipline, delegate, and interact with different kinds of people. Developing a strong sense of yourself—who you are as a person and as a leader—will both make you wise and help you develop wise people.

Authors Jim Loehr and Tony Schwartz say in their book, *Power of Full Engagement*, "Developing wise people is the next organizational frontier."

The Premise of Reinvent and Realign

The way you see yourself has everything to do with how you lead. When your view of who you are changes, so do the results you produce. Reinvent and Realign is all about becoming the person you want to be so that you can align with your values with clarity. This process will also allow you to mentor your employees to create their identities as individuals who not only empower themselves personally, but also support the team and your organization's mission.

The notion of self-reinvention is an interesting one; it's the area of personal development where you will find the most excuses and regrets until action is taken. How many people prefer the status quo even when it is detrimental to their leadership? You have probably heard the excuse "that's just the way I am" used as a way to justify rude behavior. That rude behavior may eventually lead to a lawsuit and turn into the regret of resisting change.

Eliminating excuses and regrets means aligning with your highest values so you can effectively lead others by example. Leadership is more than a title. According to Robin Sharma, one of the world's most highly respected leadership experts and author of *The Leader Who Had No Title: A Modern Fable in Real Success in Business and in Life*, "Each of us is born into genius. Sadly, most of us die amid mediocrity" (Sharma 2010, 1). What a loss of potential!

So, let me ask you: Who are you as a leader?

You might answer, "I am a vice president of operations at Community Bank," "I'm a surgeon with Mercy Hospital," or "I'm the executive director of ABC nonprofit center."

I might ask you the same question in regard to your personal life: Who are you as a person? You might answer, "I'm the mother of two beautiful children." You might also identify with the money you make, your age, or your physical appearance. This identification may not be a conscious one, but it exists and influences your actions nonetheless.

You might recognize that you have attached your identity to a particular area as you observe your feelings about those who are different from you, your reaction after you lose something you identified with, or your shift in what you value after you alter your identity.

I suggest you jot in your journal or notebook your answer to who are you question right now, to serve as your baseline as you move through this book. This is a great way to see whether this definition changes.

Do Others See You the Way You Do?

If you are not consciously aware of how you perceive yourself versus how you want to be perceived, chances are that others see you differently than you see yourself. This phenomenon can be explained by the psychological tool called *The Johari*

Window. This method—created in 1969 by American psychologists Joseph Luft and Harry Ingham—is used to help people better understand their interpersonal communication and relationships. The underlying notion is that each of our personalities is divided into these four categories (see Figure 4.1).

1. The part of ourselves that both we and others see.
2. The aspects that others see about us, but that we do not see.
3. The subconscious part of us that neither we nor others see.
4. Our private self, which we know but keep from others.

Let's have some fun with the Johari Window for a moment. Suppose you see yourself as positive and a perfectionist. Others see you that way as well. You are very proud of your leadership skills and pride yourself on being an excellent communicator. You can manage a meeting, you keep everyone on track, and you run a tight ship. You can't understand why your staff is sometimes disengaged and doesn't always cooperate with you.

There is a reason, of course—but it's not one that anyone is going to share with you. The truth is that others perceive you to

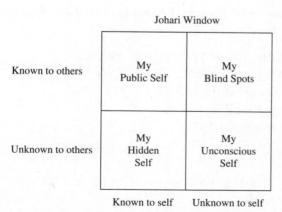

Figure 4.1   The Johari Window

be a bad listener. Therefore, they do not come to you with ideas, because they don't think it will do any good. After all, you are the boss and no one is going to risk sharing this kind of information. However, you have no idea that others experience you this way.

Let's also assume that you spent a good portion of your childhood feeling ignored. In your mind, no one ever listened to you, so in order to compensate, you learned how to get attention the only way you knew how. You overrode other people's opinions because you felt threatened when others didn't immediately accept your ideas. (This is the subconscious part of your personality—number 3 above.) You have no memory of developing this habit; it was just part of who you are.

Even though you put on a happy face, you privately feel anxiety any time you make a mistake or sense you that you're being ignored. You never let anyone see you sweat. Other people would likely be very surprised if they knew how vulnerable you feel much of the time.

Now, think about yourself. What do others know about you that you don't know? What are some subconscious patterns that show up? Are there perhaps a few areas in your life that could use some reinvention?

Does the way you view yourself keep you from doing any of the following?

- Being authentic about your unmet needs.
- Asking for what you want.
- Dishing out some straight talk to your staff.
- Absorbing feedback.
- Confronting a wrongdoing.
- Saying no.
- Taking a risk.
- Discussing a hot-button issue with a family member.
- Setting boundaries.
- Being open about who you are and what you believe.
- Reaching out for help.

- Getting the education or coaching you need.
- Advancing in your career.
- Approaching your boss.

The Tool of Awareness

Self-awareness is so vital because you can't effectively influence others unless you know yourself first. In other words, if you are unaware of who you are being in your leadership role, you will influence your team—but not necessarily in the way you want.

We relate to other people through a device in the brain called *mirror neurons.* In simple terms, we get insights into how someone else thinks and feels when we watch him or her do something. If, for example, you constantly roll your eyes or frown when talking to people, their mirror neurons will communicate to them an emotional state of disgust, disagreement, or discounting.

When I was first starting my speaking practice, I received some feedback from an audience member who informed me, "When you disagree with someone, you shake your head, interrupt, and show a little disgust on your face." Wow—I was so surprised to learn this about myself. This is an example of room number 2 in the Johari Window—an aspect of me that is apparent to others but not to me. Can you see how this unconscious pattern of mine might keep me from facilitating an effective workshop? Though my intentions were always to be of service, I was unable to make the needed shift until I became aware of the gap between my automatic patterns and my vision of myself.

Author David Rock explains in his book, *Your Brain at Work: Strategies for Overcoming Distraction, Regaining Focus, and Working Smarter All Day Long*, "Studies show that the strongest emotion in a team can ripple out and drive everyone to resonate with the same emotion without anyone consciously knowing why it is happening" (Rock 2009, 161). Leaders have an extraordinary amount of influence on their staff. It is therefore vital that they reinvent and realign to keep their actions congruent with both their vision for the company and how they want to project themselves.

The more aware you are of who you are and who you want to be, the more harmonious your attitudes, language, and behavior will be—and the more your team will trust your leadership. Are you being the person you claim to be? Do your actions align with the values you profess to have? Are you willing to abandon what doesn't fit as you tighten the gap? As you grow—both personally and professionally—you must be willing to fine-tune this approach to assure that who you are matches who you want to be.

The question "who am I?" is one of the most important questions you will ever face. And it's a question you likely will ask yourself periodically throughout your life as your roles and circumstances change.

When people go through a significant career transition, such as losing a job, or retiring from a rewarding career, they often suffer an identity crisis. Who you think you are now may not be who you think you are five years from now.

At different times in life, I have thought I knew exactly who I am. I have identified with accomplishments, awards, and my job. I have been a title-holding bodybuilder, a factory worker, a professional speaker, an author, and the founder of Stop Your Drama. I have been contemplating the "who am I?" question ever since I was first asked—and my idea of who I am keeps changing.

If you have thought deeply about your life, how your career and professional personas go together, and the roles you play—then you've also probably had this dialogue with yourself. If not, then you are getting ready to do so for the first time.

Who Do You Think You Are?

Just as we relate to others through our mirror neurons, we discover who we are through the mirror of relationship. Dr. David Simon, author of *Free to Love, Free to Heal: Heal Your Body by Healing Your Emotions*, teaches the principle of healing your body by healing your emotions. In 1996, Dr. Simon partnered with world-renowned spiritual teacher

Deepak Chopra to open the Chopra Center for Wellbeing in order to help people experience physical healing, emotional freedom, and higher states of consciousness. Dr. Simon makes the claim that we learn as children who we are from the responses we get from the adults in our lives (Simon 2009, 4).

And of course, these adults have often had their own problems; therefore, we tend to receive a distorted mirror image of ourselves. At this early point in life, we haven't yet developed the maturity or critical thinking skills to say "Hey, this isn't about me. It must be their problem."

The nurturing you received during your childhood helped you create a story of who you are—and that story continues to support your abilities or struggles as a leader to this day. In some ways, all of us have looked through a distorted mirror at one point or another. That is why it is important to now decide who we choose to be, rather than continuing to live by a story that others have created about us.

Despite our upbringing or the way in which we've learned to view ourselves until now, we can perfect the looking glass so that we see ourselves more clearly from here on in—and that clarity will allow us to see others more clearly. When you see who you truly are, you begin to alter the behavior and habits that no longer serve you, and start observing other people differently as well. Eventually, you become better able to help and guide those around you to find their own clarity.

If you want to be clearer about who you think you are, consider your choices and actions every day, as well as how you represent yourself. Remember the LABOR Principles I spoke about earlier: Listen, Ask for What You Want, Boundaries, Own Your Stuff, and Represent Yourself. You represent yourself every day whether or not you mean to.

Habits, Reactions, and Conscious Choices

All of us operate from programmed habits as well as from deliberate and conscious choice. For example, perhaps you consciously choose to style your hair, put on makeup, take enough business cards, and prepare your "elevator speech" for a business meeting you're attending. You are representing yourself as a professional, and that becomes your intention.

Then, when a group of people gather to talk, perhaps you continue to interrupt, share your point of view, and exclude others standing in the perimeters. Although you are unaware of the habits you project and may well see yourself as professional, you represent yourself as someone who is self-engaged, rude, and obnoxious. No matter how you justify or excuse your own behaviors, others will interpret them in a particular way and add meaning to their interpretations.

Be honest with yourself about the habits you possess, both positive and negative. Sometimes, this requires that you give up habits that no longer serve you. As we discussed in Principle 1, clearing the fog can help. As I mentioned before, when I got clear that my mission was to improve communication and relationships, I decided to quit using reactions like sarcasm and eye rolling as defensive mechanisms. I also worked on my listening skills. Those habits were not easy to change—but doing so helped serve me incredibly well in the long run.

Don't Confuse Where You Are with Who You Are

As I slowly came to realize that I was less effective as a leader than I wanted to be, I often judged myself harshly. I was living in the gap—an experience that made me temporarily uncomfortable. I learned an important lesson from that experience: Don't confuse where you are with who you are. Even if you struggle in your leadership position—if you sometimes come on too strong, weak, opinionated, or decisive—*who you are* is more powerful than *where you are*. Now that you are beginning to see that you want to change, you may be uncomfortable with what you see in yourself; but don't let that stop you. Keep rowing toward that change, even if you aren't there yet. Keep your eye on the island, even if you are in choppy waters.

Digging deeper will help you uncover some of the things that feed your negative habits—which will lead you to clues that can help you change. You may, for example, realize that you often assume you won't be heard at all if you aren't aggressive. This essentially means that you don't consider yourself important enough for others to listen to. In order to represent yourself consciously, you must be aware of how others will interpret your behaviors and actions—and then consciously choose them. You must, in this case, make the adult decision that no one wants to listen to an interrupting bully—but that many will take the advice of someone who is considerate and clear in her communications. Then you must act to change this habit.

If you lead others and keep covering for your staff's mistakes; or you're hiding information from your own boss, board of directors, or whomever you're accountable to, then your impression of yourself is one who must rescue others or hide information. It might also mean that you see your superiors as people who will not help you or understand your dilemma, or, perhaps you are in denial. In that case, you probably don't consider yourself to be strong enough to handle the truth. But—if you change either how you see yourself or how you see others, your entire situation will change. If you stay in denial, things will only get worse. Start to observe the various segments of your life, and you will learn a lot.

If in your workplace you are always the one staying overtime, sacrificing to fill in the gaps, feeling resentful or being taken advantage of, I can make an educated guess about what you think of yourself and what you think of your colleagues, team members, or boss. I can also hear the justifications: "It doesn't do any good to ask for help," or "If I don't do it, it won't get done," to "That's just what is expected of me." If you want to discover what obstacles are standing in your way, listen for the explanations, justifications, and how you define yourself.

You have to be willing to see yourself differently to facilitate different results. Whatever you choose to focus on will expand. The island will get closer if you concentrate on moving ahead.

"I Am" Equals My Truth

A great awareness exercise to see who you think you are is to listen consciously to the ways you use the phrase "I am."

You will learn a lot about your staff by the way they describe themselves using the "I am" phrase. *I am a neat freak. I am frustrated. I am a worrier. I am a people person. I am a perfectionist.* One of my favorite books is *The Four Agreements: A Pratical Guide to Personal Freedom, A Toltec Wisdom Book*, in which author Don Miguel Ruiz asserts that the first agreement is to be impeccable with your word. Talking badly about yourself is an act of self-betrayal (Ruiz 1997, 25, 31).

You will learn a lot about yourself if you are willing to keep a journal for just one week and record the ways you use the phrase "I am." My friend Jocelyn, who created a new identity around a career as a writer and editor, recalls the leadership she received from a college professor: "A writing professor I had in college told us to tell others, 'I am a writer' to help us to create this new reality. I found usefulness in this exercise of prematurely using the language to describe the 'I am' that I wanted in my life."

Reinventing a Strong Sense of Self in the Workplace

How might you use this same exercise to challenge one of your staff members to reinvent a new "I am" reality?

A frontline leader named Emma with whom I used to work was not a supervisor but was in a leadership position, since she was—as status in the factory would have it—right under the supervisor and right above the other line workers. As odd as it might sound, Emma was actually proud of her inability to get along with others. "I can be a bitch," she would say with a twinkle in her eyes. "Yes, I can," she would conclude, almost as a warning to others not to mess with her. In fact, I recall that one time she offered to take me out into the parking lot to "beat me up" (an invitation I declined). Then she sat with me 30 minutes later on a scheduled break and acted as if the conversation had never happened.

Bullying at work is a real problem. If you have a self-proclaimed bitch on your staff, be aware that she is a lawsuit just waiting to happen. But what might happen if you could inspire this person to reinvent? Of course, she must first desire change and see it as a benefit to her status, opportunities for advancement, or some other personal goal. Otherwise, you will only get resistance.

I have worked with a number of leaders who need to soften their communication skills, and who often justify their tendencies by claiming "That's just the way I am." They are consistently ready to cite their inability to change; occasionally, they've taken a personality test to provide a good excuse for why they are an innate bully. Well, that's *the story*; let's look at *the facts*. Did you know the number one reason for turnover is the boss-employee relationship—and that most employees' number one fear is an overly aggressive boss who uses intimidation tactics to get things done?

The ways we define ourselves frequently offer the very excuses we need not to change. Take, for example, the "I am a perfectionist" or "I am a people pleaser" definition. I have worked with professionals who waste a lot of time reworking, reorganizing and redoing project after project because of their need to be perfect. They claim to be perfectionists who pride themselves on doing excellent work. I've also coached individuals who label themselves as people pleasers and who, as a result, are always exhausted from sacrificing their time to make sure everyone else's needs are met.

Labels and Self–Definition Justify Unmet Needs

It's quite clear that the way we identify and label ourselves has everything to do with how we work as a team, lead, and interact with others. Much of the time, we have created a story about who we are to justify an unmet need.

If you refer to yourself as a bitch, then you get to have an excuse for being rude instead of risking being vulnerable and asking someone else to stop something offensive. If you're a self-proclaimed people person, then you get to blame others for your exhaustion rather than risk the relationship by saying "no" and dealing honestly with someone else's disappointment. If you declare you're a perfectionist, you create a reason for being too busy to accept an invitation—and you also protect yourself from any criticism that could come your way if your work needs editing or improvement.

A simple shift in your identity might help you make friends, eliminate the users from your life, and have more time to do what you really want to do. But unfortunately, if you are like most of us, you would rather be right.

Myths about Self-Reinvention

Instead of making the necessary changes from the inside, we believe that we must wait for the circumstance first in order to change. For example, *I will become a better communicator when I get the promotion. I will start taking care of my appearance when I meet the right person. I will get the certification when I get a new title*. However, this is a myth—and a dangerous one, at that. You must change first—and then the right circumstance for growth will present itself.

I used to believe in these myths myself. Before I ever left the factory I told myself, "When I become a professional, then I'll be able to communicate effectively." So, the excuse was, "I don't have to improve right where I am. I will wait until . . . ."

I call this myth "salvation on the island." So many people think that once they arrive on the island, they will find fulfillment, live on purpose, communicate better, become a leader—fill in the blank. Perhaps you can even see yourself or someone you work with here: *When I get another boss, then it will be easy. After I fire this one employee, then the team will row together. Once I get my certification, then the problems will be solved*. But all that believing in this myth does is allow more excuses to be made.

Excuses Always Inhibit Personal Growth

People tend to use time most frequently as an excuse for procrastination. "When I get the time, then I will . . ." But guess what—you have to make the decision first. Then the time, resources, and people will appear and help you get to the island.

However, getting to the island is still an illusion. Though it's fun and rewarding, the relief is only temporary. A more valuable solution is to step into a new truth and step into a new identity

Stepping into a New Identity

How can you empower employees who are still operating based on excuses? One approach is to encourage them to accept a new truth about themselves and see the power of a new identity. When you see yourself the way you want to be, you can simply claim ownership of the new identity.

Once when I was traveling, I stayed at a Ritz-Carlton in one city, then at another hotel two days later in another city. The distinctions even in the manners of the staff were astounding. At the Ritz-Carlton, every employee seemed to have a high esteem and sense of pride—because no matter what their job description or responsibility, they have an identity of being "ladies and gentlemen serving ladies and gentlemen"—the official Ritz-Carlton motto as posted on their web site, ritzcarlton.com.

The Ritz-Carlton hotel chain operates based on 12 service values, some of which build strong identities among all who are employed there. For example, "I am proud of my professional language, appearance and behavior" and, "I own and immediately resolve guest problems." It's easy to see how just those two service values would prohibit irresponsible behavior or excuses such as "It's not my job." In fact, when I commented to a hotel employee on how accommodating they were, the man who was setting up my room gave me a copy of the service values, motto, and employee promise—all contained on a quad-fold miniature brochure which every employee carries in his or her pocket and commits to memory.

My encouragement to anyone seeking positive change is this: You can do it—and the time is now. Don't wait to get to the island. Be who you want to be right this second. Give yourself permission to be excellent, and stop letting others define you. If you need to clean up some old baggage or make amends to move on, then do it now—so you can be proud of who you are now instead of making excuses for who you could have been. In fact, no matter what your previous experiences have been or how you have behaved, your past does not have to equal your future. You can start reinventing and be successful today right from where you are.

I love the following concept that author Eckhart Tolle, in his book *A New Earth: Awakening to Your Life's Purpose*, has introduced concerning success: "Don't let a mad world tell you success is anything other than a successful present moment. You cannot achieve success; you can only be successful" (Tolle 2006, 270). Doesn't that take the pressure off? Success is a state of being, just like the fact that you are a woman or a man. You can't seek that which you already are.

The four questions you must ask yourself are:

1. Who am I?
2. What am I committed to?
3. What actions and behaviors are out of alignment with who I say I am?
4. As a leader am I getting my desired results?

Since you already asked yourself the first two questions in the last chapter, you should already know what you want. Now ask yourself the next two: are you taking a left-hand turn to the island called "excuses," or are you rowing straight to the island called "leadership"? From there, you start reinventing and realigning. Each word, behavior, and habit ultimately shines the light on where you really are, and whether your deeds match your thoughts and words.

Keep track of all the ways you define yourself, and correct yourself when you are misaligned with your word. As a result, you'll have a great relationship with yourself—something that becomes the foundation for your relationship with others.

Your Staff's Turn

Chances are that you're also seeking better results from your staff. In order to do so, you must also help them reinvent and realign. Do not try to strong-arm them with command and control tactics. Use power—not force. No one is motivated to offer his best when his leader doesn't inspire him or see his potential. As I've mentioned, people want to work for purpose, not just a paycheck. They're naturally motivated to succeed if they receive the right tools and right environment.

Motivation is about more than just money. Speaker and author of *Firsthand Lessons, Secondhand Dogs: Living, Laboring, Learning . . . and Letting Go,* Scott Carbonara, tells a story about his experience working in human resources at a major health insurance company experiencing a high attrition rate. His boss had decided that the company would start offering monetary incentives for those who would stick with the company. However, Carbonara believed that money wasn't the answer to the attrition problem, as he had heard comments from former workers such as, "I would cry all the way to work, and all the way home from work each day." He asked his boss to reconsider the stay bonuses and instead address the reasons why people were leaving—and his boss agreed. Carbonara was promoted to chief of staff, where he was able to contribute to dropping the attrition rate from 38 percent to just over 6 percent within a few years. He helped improve communication and address the issues that had hindered employees from becoming and feeling engaged (Carbonara 2010, 55–56).

Assuming that your hiring systems are adequate and that you've recruited individuals with the potential to help you row your boat to the right island, then you must begin seeing your staff as the capable, brilliant people that they are. Your next step is to give them the coaching and tools they need to turn their boats toward this vision. Stop viewing them as incompetent, complaining, whining, and helpless troublemakers—even if that's how you see them right now. You must understand that who they are is not the same as how they are behaving.

How to Help Your Team Reinvent and Realign

Most of us are looking for acceptance—someone or something to tell us we are worthy. However, what we really need is to look in the mirror and tell this very thing to ourselves. If you can first do some of this validating work yourself, it will be easier to teach it to your staff. I truly believe that because I have done everything I teach, I am able to reach people more quickly. They know that I have done the work myself, and that I'm experiencing many of the same things they are.

Suppose you have a team member who wants to be promoted to the next level of her career path: office manager. Coach your employee a little, and ask her questions like: How might an office manager dress and behave? What skills do you think an office manager might need to have? Then help that person to identify the gaps that she has. If she does not recognize them herself, give her some time to figure it out; have her create a list and give it to you. If, for example, Sally wants the promotion but turns down every opportunity she is given to go to a conference to learn a new skill, you should tell Sally what you have observed. If Robert is resentful because he got passed up for a promotion but is constantly late to meetings, explain why he missed out on this opportunity. Be gentle but firm in your explanations. Express to your employees the requirements of the jobs they want—for instance, to be self-motivated and self-directed. They may not know what is expected unless it is pointed out. For example, ask if you can give feedback on how your staff members represent themselves when they arrive late, and how this impacts the rest of the team. Stick to the facts, and do not make it personal. Ask a simple question such as, "If you were leading others, what advice would you give to someone who has trouble being on time?" or, "How do you think tardiness could impact your opportunities, or impact the entire team?" Then wait for the answer. This type of communication is respectful and nonthreatening when done correctly. Then follow up by asking for the behavior you want: "I want you to arrive on time to meetings prepared to share your ideas."

Until employees learn how to be totally responsible, it is our job as leaders to guide their thinking. If your employees resist hearing the truth when you speak it kindly but directly, then maybe they are not ready for the promotions. Perhaps they have some of their own drama work yet to do.

Ask your employees if they want feedback when you see a gap or behaviors that are out of alignment with what they claim are their goals. This gives them choice in the matter and the chance to get rewarded for asking for help. Better yet, ask them to evaluate themselves on a regular basis. People are more conscious when they're compelled to be honest about their own strengths and areas needing improvement. If you can elicit this kind of cooperation, you are training them to be aware of the skills and behaviors that are expected of them in order to advance their careers. Now you are on the same team, rowing together to help promote within.

Try to catch and discourage self-deprecating talk among your team members. If you hear someone saying, "I must be so stupid," gently correct him and try to get him to see it differently. If possible, design a team development meeting to discuss the importance of self-respect and positive language. You can even make a game out of it to help everyone develop congruent language and actions.

Combining Individual Visions with the Company Vision

A substantial problem can occur when you know who you are but are not completely aligned with your company's vision and mission. Feeling misaligned in your career can create a lot of internal drama. You have to find some way to align your role as a leader with who your company wants you to be. You cannot successfully work for a company or with a team that threatens your core values. Well, you can, but your health and sanity will suffer. Think of various politicians' staff members who have been involved in scandal and eventually resigned. How many later revealed the ways they had to compromise their values to keep their jobs?

It's encouraging to know that even if you work in a drama-laden environment, you can influence those even in higher positions of power—or, at the very least, stay steadfast in your own direction—as long as you can increase your own clarity sufficiently enough. Remember, the one with clarity navigates the ship. If you absolutely must work in an environment that is not as team-oriented or people-friendly as you'd like, you can still get clear on who you are and how you perform, and eliminate excuses that do not empower you. Your clarity will be contagious—I guarantee it.

The information that I am sharing with you now—as well as the entirety of the Stop Your Drama Methodology, and every piece of the work I currently do—was accomplished because I created a clear vision of who I wanted to be in this world. I experienced this transformation after learning about the Karpman Drama Triangle (which I share with you in Chapter 5), and when I learned about the power of taking responsibility for all the components in my world.

I believe this work is so empowering because I used these principles at the lowest level of the factory floor. At that time, I did not have a degree; I did not have a powerful position or prestige. When I started changing my vision of myself from disempowered factory worker to someone committed to improving communication and relationships, I had no idea what kind of work was in store for me. But I knew that I was going to move in that direction.

Remember the gap? Well, I had a huge emotional and spiritual gap to close. After all, I had developed automatic internal programming about the workplace and power. I was hanging on to the old story of "them versus us," all of which was as alive and well in my head as it was on the factory floors.

Faulty Thinking

You might be thinking a number of things right now: "This will never work for me," "You don't know my employees," "This won't work because of all the changes we have been through," or even, "This sounds very idealistic, and not applicable in the real world." If you're thinking this way, you probably feel stuck. This book has not yet offered the solution you were seeking.

When you are stuck, you suffer. One of my favorite authors, James Allen, says in his book, *As A Man Thinketh*, "Suffering is always the effect of wrong thought in some direction" (Allen 1992, 17). If you are suffering through this material—or if you believe that what I say is true for me but not necessarily for you—then read on and see if your thinking changes.

I also had faulty thinking when I first started to apply these principles. I thought to myself, "I will improve communication and relationships everywhere, after I am a professional. After all, I can't do it as a factory worker. Plus, my boss is very stubborn, and you can't reason with a rock."

Now you can see in print how I viewed myself (as a factory worker versus professional), and how I viewed my supervisor (as a rock who couldn't listen to reason). I can guarantee you that had I asked around to get approval, I could have found enough people to agree with my logic. However, we tend to seek social proof to prove the opinions we already hold—so that we can be right. This need to be right keeps us from stepping into a new truth and creating a new story.

I was fortunate, however. As I meditated on this problem, I realized that if I could not live these principles on the factory floor, I would not have the credibility to teach them to others later. I speak from experience and power that these principles do work in any area of your life. With time, I gathered the courage to have some authentic conversations with my boss, and everything changed. This newfound courage evolved because I started seeing myself differently, not because I was yet a skilled communicator. I simply began to view myself as a professional—even though I was still on the factory floor—and I started shifting my perception of my boss to see him as someone who was just doing the best he could with his level of knowledge and the workload put upon him. Once I considered myself to be a partner instead of a competitor, everything started changing—for the better.

Questions to Answer

1. Who am I?
2. What am I committed to?
3. What actions and behaviors are out of alignment with who I say I am?
4. As a leader, am I getting my desired results?

Learning Points

- Who you think you are will influence your leadership style.
- We learn who we are through the mirror of relationship.
- Change takes time. Who you are is more powerful than where you are.
- To get different results, see yourself differently.
- "I am" equals my truth.
- If you do not trust yourself, you cannot act in your best interests.
- Getting your basic needs met is essential for good leadership.

Chapter 5

Stop Relationship Drama

*If it's very painful for you to criticize your friends—you're
safe in doing it. But if you take the slightest pleasure in it,
that's the time to hold your tongue.*

—Alice Duer Miller

Besides a lack of clarity, all drama has a relationship component. When I first started my business as a professional speaker, I had a lot of drama. Business was not as good as I wanted it to be, so I hired a coach.

After some digging, the coach uncovered something that was significantly impeding my growth: I did not like the phone. I avoided making follow-up calls, and cold calls were completely out of the question. So, my coach said something that changed my life: "Marlene, if you want to excel at this business, you need to fall in love with the phone."

I jokingly say today that this was the best relationship advice I have ever received. The point is, the only way you experience anything is in relationship to something else. I had a bad relationship with the phone, and it kept me from doing things that I needed to do to make my business succeed.

The Premise of Stop Relationship Drama Is This

Everything in life is centered on relationships, and relationships exist because of the way in which you think. You can only experience someone or some situation in relationship to yourself; therefore, in order to change anything in your life, you must change the way you think about it. When you are willing to see another person differently, you can change your relationship with that person.

One of my favorite quotes by motivational author Terry Josephson is, "No matter where you go or what you do, you live your entire life within the confines of your head."

Relationships are always active first on the nonphysical level. In other words, they exist because of your thinking. You can't even have a relationship with someone until you think about that person, right? When you first meet someone, you form an impression, and your views of that person build and shift as you interact with and observe him or her. In essence, your thoughts influence your behaviors—and thus, your relationship—toward that person.

We talked about your relationship with yourself in the previous chapter—who you think you are, what you think you are capable of, and how you know yourself to be. When your thoughts about yourself change, so does your experience.

But what about all the other relationships you have—to time, money, your past, your imagined future, your body, and every other aspect of your life? Let's look at a short list of relationships you currently have. You might even want to write about these in a journal to get more of a handle on how they influence your life.

- ◆ Your present situation
- ◆ Your past
- ◆ Your perceived future
- ◆ Your spouse or significant other
- ◆ Your family members
- ◆ Your coworkers
- ◆ Money
- ◆ Food
- ◆ Fitness
- ◆ Politics
- ◆ The holidays
- ◆ Religion

The list is as long as the experiences, people, and other elements in your life. According to best-selling author of *Conversations with God: An Uncommon Dialogue*, Neale Donald Walsch, the real question we answer every day is: "Who am I in relationship to that?" The "that" we are talking about in this chapter is your relationship with others—whether they're your employees, your coworkers, or your boss.

Why Relationships Matter

Your success and ultimately your happiness in life are directly related to the quality and quantity of your relationships. The more connected you feel, the happier you are.

This is equally true in your workplace. Research company Gallup reports on their web site that having one good friend at work is essential for employee satisfaction. Good workplace relationships are simply good business. Why? Because nine out of ten problems that employees encounter at work are people-related. Therefore, you have solved nine out of ten problems when you focus on developing better workplace relationships between colleagues.

No matter what your role, the way you see others will impact your relationship with them. Author David Rock's *Your Brain at Work* introduces studies that show how we create images about our own and others' status in the brain when we communicate with them (Rock 2010). These images influence how we treat and interact with them. If, for instance, you view your employees or your boss with an "us against them" mentality, it will reveal itself in your communication—even if you think you are hiding it.

I will never forget the time during one of my previous jobs when a business unit manager sat with the hourly employees at the break table. No one said anything the entire time, and he was treated like an outsider because we did not see him as one of us. Unsurprisingly, this hurt his feelings—and he expressed it.

The "us against them" mentality is alive and well from factories to banks, from front line employees to CEOs. So, if you want to interact with someone in a new or different way, you have to transform the way in which you view him. Change the relationships, and you change the culture.

As a leader or manager, you have a lot more influence to change the relationship culture than you might think. The primary relationship at work is that between boss and employee (Levering and Urbanska 1996). In fact, Gallup's employee engagement research found that no single factor more clearly or accurately predicts an employee's productivity than his relationship with his direct supervisor. It's comparable to a parent-child relationship, where the primary influencer in the home is the parent. If there is lots of drama between the kids, there is probably a problem with the parent. However, when the two parents are aligned and clear, the children are generally more cooperative. The same principles apply in the workplace. Strong leadership and a solid relationship with your employees promote healthy work habits and high levels of engagement and productivity. As a leader, you will have to face a serious challenge that will test your principles at some point. This challenge may be to confront a difficult relationship issue in the workplace. You may feel divided over the need to keep the peace or talk to an employee who is slacking off. Or, your dilemma may be the need to keep someone in a higher position happy and sacrifice your values. You may have to choose to stand true to who you are and risk disappointing someone, or losing the relationship with a colleague altogether. The way you see people will determine your ability to inspire and get others to collaborate with the team.

This point came to light for me while I was watching reality show *Undercover Boss* one evening. In this particular episode, Hooters CEO Colby Brooks went undercover to work at the bottom rung of the company in an effort to learn more about the corporate culture, people, perceptions, customer service, and how the team worked together. Upon arriving at one of his franchises in Texas, Brooks immediately realized that the restaurant manager was labeling the waitresses as prima donnas—people he felt he had to degrade in order to get their respect.

Disguised as a new hire, Brooks witnessed the manager degrade the girls by making them play a game called "Reindeer Games" to decide which got to go home early on a slow day. The girls were made to compete by eating a plate of beans with no silverware while standing up and bending down to the table with hands clasped behind their backs. Needless to say, the CEO had to use extreme restraint not to break his cover and put a stop to the mismanagement. However, he realized that the manager's inappropriate behavior resulted from the way he viewed his staff in relationship to the way he viewed himself. If the manager had seen his waitstaff as valuable and intelligent partners, he would have never made the same error.

We treat people according to how we view them. Whether you are a parent, manager, or business owner, your job as a leader is to first see yourself as a person of value, so that whatever you experience from others does not come across as a threat to your esteem. Operating from this place of security will make you less apt to react in ways that could harm the company or its members. Second, you must see the potential and speak to the highest and best version of the person you are mentoring or leading. In other words, you must learn how to honor the person and discount the story; otherwise, you will get trapped on the Drama Triangle.

The Drama Triangle

I first learned about the Drama Triangle when I was undergoing my own reinvention and transformation, and looking for answers to the "who am I?" question. The Drama Triangle actually changed my life and is partly responsible for where I am today. In fact, "Stop Your Drama" was named after the Drama Triangle.

The Drama Triangle has been an instrumental tool for more than three decades. It's been used by professional counselors and psychologists across the country, and is now being utilized in leadership training by myself and David Emerald, author of *The Power of TED: The Empowerment Dynamic*. The model was first developed in 1968 by Dr. Stephen Karpman, a highly respected psychiatrist known for his contributions to transactional analysis—an area in which he was awarded the Eric Berne Scientific Award for Options for his work.

The concept as I teach it is this. When relationships are dysfunctional, there are three basic roles that people play: persecutor, rescuer, and victim. (For some, it is easier to think of the roles on the Triangle as archetypes.) The diagram, as Dr. Karpman originally developed it, is an equilateral upside-down triangle. On each point of the triangle lie the dys-functional roles that people play. For the purposes of this book, the victim is considered to be someone who is always in the one-down position, sees no choice, and has no sense of empowerment.

Simplified Snapshot

Per the Karpman Triangle model, the victim feels helpless, the rescuer has the answer, and the persecutor tells you whose fault it is. So, if you have an employee who constantly plays the victim role, you will likely hear stories about why life is hard or unfair, or constant complaints and excuses why they are unable to change. This fundamental belief helps the employees create and support self-defeating patterns that prove that they are right—life really is hard—and keep them stuck in their current roles.

The victim pattern can be subtle and sometimes difficult to recognize, even if you are a very responsible person overall. I had many victim beliefs when I worked in the factory before starting my professional career. It was difficult for me to even imagine having a different career—a belief that kept me from even attempting to attend college until I was in my thirties.

When people first learn about the Triangle, they find that they identify with a particular role. Most leaders identify most with the rescuer role; after all, in order to be a leader, you can't be operating from the victim orientation every day.

An overview of each of the roles is given below. See with which one you identify most as you think about your relation-ships and the areas where you experience drama. Let's start with the rescuer role.

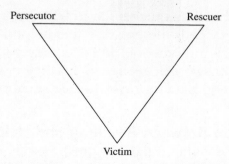

Figure 5.1 The Karpman Drama Triangle

The Rescuer Role

The rescuer role reveals itself in subtle ways and brings with it the need to make things right, fix problems, or take ownership of issues that don't belong to you. It shows up as feeling caught in the middle, drained from resentment, and as though you're never able to offer enough. It elicits the impression that no one can solve a given problem except you.

Rescue tendencies can be mixed with a true desire to help and are common in those of us who like to control the show or make sure we are using time wisely. I feel it arising in myself when a meeting gets out of hand or goes overtime. I notice the rescuer in me trying to emerge as I feel the almost irresistible urge to step in and take charge. Because I'm competent at keeping a meeting on track, I can become irritated when I'm involved in one that gets out of hand. This level of awareness helps me to understand what is happening when I feel the urge to rescue. If I am not the chair of the meeting, I must choose to act differently and relinquish my role as rescuer.

The same principle exists when parents take over a task that they are trying to teach their children, or with a teacher who struggles to be patient with a slow learner. It is often difficult to sit by and watch someone less competent than yourself as he learns a new skill. While leading is the only way to empower, rescuing still provides a quicker fix. In addition, rescuing makes us feel good and feeds the ego. We feel helpful and important when we're rescuing someone, and even develop the belief that we have all the answers or are a hero in a time of need. Rescuing is a fairly common pattern in workplace situations.

The Distinction Between Rescuing and Helping

It can initially be difficult to distinguish between rescuing and helping. This can create some unnecessary drama; after all, you don't want to refuse to help when someone really needs a hand. However, the difference here is the energetic charge or the emotional component. Feeling resentful that someone did not take your advice is a sign that you were rescuing and not helping. On the other hand, when you help, you do so because it is a representation of who you are. You do not need to be the hero, because you are helping out of a desire to be of assistance.

When someone asks for your input or guidance, project a little in advance to see how you will feel if you help.

If you keep helping a coworker and his performance just keeps spiraling down, it's time to hold off and set some boundaries. When you help a coworker and your help is returned as a favor, or when the help was an out-of-the-ordinary request, then you probably feel good about it. This truly was helping, instead of covering for incompetence.

On the other hand, keeping vital information from someone whom you are trying to keep happy is rescuing—versus risking a disagreement so you can have an authentic communication that will eventually clear the air.

How Rescuing Manifests in Business

Rescuing is rampant in business. Managers hide information from their bosses because they believe they are not stable enough to handle it. Undisclosed deals are made to keep information from Annie because it will hurt her feelings if we tell her she isn't stepping up to the plate. Instead of embracing transparency, managers keep secrets because they see their employees as victims who wouldn't understand the problem—instead of team players who could help solve it.

Whether it's the worker who always stays late for everyone else, the boss who continues to cover for a bad employee, or the CFO who skews the numbers in order to meet standards, rescuing is as alive and well on Main Street as it is on Wall Street. Those of us in leadership positions most likely find ourselves acting from the rescuer role more often than not. Read on if you want ideas on how to cease doing so.

How to Eliminate Rescuing Tendencies

The first thing you have to do is get clear on your intended outcome and own the truth about why you believe the task at hand can't be completed without you or someone else's approval. According to *Change Your Thinking, Change Your Life: How to Unlock Your Full Potential for Success and Achievement* author Brian Tracy, "Nothing and no one can have control over you unless there is something you still want from them" (Tracy 2003). Sometimes we simply want approval or the knowledge that we have the power to change others.

Second, you have to quit being responsible for everyone else's life and be responsible to your own—or as my husband used to say, understand that you are not the controller of the universe.

Third, you must try to consciously see those around you differently. You must honor the people, and discount the story they might currently believe about themselves. By doing this, you raise their status and self-esteem. If you view them as capable, you might have to be willing to let them suffer (just a little) the consequences of their decisions, instead of always carrying their load for them. After all, would you always step in so quickly if you really thought they were capable? It's true that their feelings may be a bit hurt when you shift and start speaking authentically, and I definitely recommend being kind in your approach. However, ask yourself: Are you rowing to the island called "keeping you comfortable" or are you rowing to the island called "authentic relationship"?

The two real questions here are: Do you trust yourself to deliver your truth in a kind way? And do you trust others to be mature enough to handle your truth? If not (and take a deep breath), you don't have a real relationship anyway.

Enforce Your Rules

You must be consistent with your rules when you're leading others—whether they're spoken rules or documented in a handbook. One particularly helpful strength-building exercise is to learn how to set a boundary, or to say no in a kind way without apologizing—or without an anger reaction if they don't adhere to your request. This is much more difficult than it sounds, especially if others are used to manipulating you or see you as sweet and kind. We will talk more about boundaries as a way to master your energy. For now, focus on the lessons in this chapter and learn to identify the roles on the Triangle when they manifest.

Rescuer Checklist

1. Difficulty saying no.
2. Fighting other people's battles, and/or mending other people's arguments.
3. Allowing people to frequently borrow money from you.
4. Taking care of adult kids who are capable and competent.
5. Getting angry when people don't take your advice.
6. Hiding information from people because you think they can't handle it.
7. Believing that you know it all.
8. Feeling superior and more competent than those around you.
9. Sacrificing your needs in favor of others'.
10. Obsessing about other people's problems.

Why Most of Us Identify with the Rescuer Role

It feels better to be a rescuer than to be a victim, and the persecutor seems like the mean position to be in. It's much more preferable to help, and at first glance, rescuing looks like help.

If you are still convinced that rescuing is a beneficial role, then consider the final outcome: The rescuer role keeps you in hopeless relationships, a career that you have outgrown, or on a committee you no longer have use for. You're usually covering for a bully, or letting employee transgressions slide without confronting the problem. Eventually, your body or emotions will warn you that you have had enough. You will feel resentful, exhausted, taken advantage of, and misunderstood.

When you think about it, that sounds more like a victim. Once you have rescued to your limits, you start to feel defeated and fail to recognize the choices around you. You build a story around why you can't have an authentic conversation with the staff, or why your executive manager will never go for your new idea to have regular employee meetings each month. In fact, when you wake up from rescuing, you feel like the victim.

The Victim Role

Because you are human and may not have been aware of some of your intentions, your victim role manifests in your life at various times—even if you are an otherwise responsible individual. When you feel helpless, trapped, depressed and can't see any way to break free, you will know you have fallen to the bottom point of the Triangle: the victim role. We will talk about what to do when you succumb to the victim role; but first, let's look at how to recognize victims in your workplace.

How to Identify Victim Behaviors in Your Staff

The victim complains. The victim loves an audience, whether of one or many. The fact is, complaining never solves a problem; it is just a spotlight for drama.

Sometimes it is difficult to know how to manage an employee who is a complainer; after all, you do want open communication, and it is appropriate to help people to feel heard so they can process and move on. However, having an open door to hear incessant complaining does not equal good listening skills.

One way to spot the victim in your staff is to notice that he or she usually doesn't want options or choices that will promote or enable change. The victim simply wants to be right. When you try to counsel an employee who is like this, you will hear versions of the tunes "But you just don't understand" and "I don't have any choices."

There may well be a kernel of truth in what you are hearing; the work may be difficult, or the situation may be unfair. However, while it's tempting to get hooked into the story, you must discount their claims and stand firm on seeing the employee as one who can discover choice.

Giving advice rarely works when someone is in victim mode. Let's face it; most of us do not like being told what to do, especially when we are emotionally stuck. When people have begun operating in the victim mode, they experience some degree of satisfaction of holding on to the rightness of their drama. Therefore, no matter what solution you offer, they simply will not accept your ideas. First of all, they want to be right. Second, their status is threatened when you have the answer, because they've already built a case around why they're right—and your claims challenge their belief system. If you keep trying to offer feedback and solutions, I can guarantee you the victim will push your buttons; you will turn into a persecutor because you will be so angry at their inability to appreciate your efforts.

What to Do to Minimize Victim Behavior

You want to teach your staff to come prepared to identify the problem, and to have at least an idea or partial solution that involves their active participation. When you create a culture of asking for what you want instead of complaining about what you don't want, your productivity will drastically increase and you won't be spending your time putting out fires.

When you ask the question "What are your choices?" you will know whether you are speaking to an empowered employee or a victim. The victim will always say, "I don't have any choices."

Avoid the tendency to rescue, but remain kind and firm. "Jason, you are a capable and intelligent guy. I have seen your creativity in times of stress. What I want from you is to go take a short break, get a drink of water, and go back to work. Are you willing to come back in an hour? If you need to, you can sleep on it, and then come back to me with a few possibilities."

Promote Empowerment

The empowered employee who is ready to take ownership will either come up with some possible choices, or at least be willing to see the light with a little help from you. When the time comes to resume the conversation, you can use the power of questions to help Jason gain clarity and relinquish the role of victim. When Jason keeps talking about what is not fair and what he doesn't want, turn the tables and ask him to answer this question: What do you want?

He may just come up with more story. If so, interrupt gently and say, "Jason, I understand the problems. My question is, 'What do you want?'" If he can name what he wants, then you've won half the battle. Your leadership can help him map out a plan or create some alternative choices. If the employee is determined to remain in the victim role, your job is to set some boundaries and guide him to see the choices. Just remember as you are trying to facilitate positive change—often, people secretly enjoy some of the payoffs of being a victim. They get attention or feel loved when others feel sorry for them, or they get to play out their drama and distract everyone else from productivity.

What we have just introduced with Jason's situation is coaching skills. Coaching involves the ability to detach from the person's drama, hold him in respect, and help him gain clarity and choice. As I mentioned above, it is never about the solution in the beginning. There is an energetic component going on. A solution would take the victim off the Triangle and out of the spotlight. If your employee avoids solutions and consistently says there is no choice, it's probably going to be time for a heart-to-heart, authentic conversation. You don't want to be silent about negativity; it is as contagious as a virus. You must address any bitterness associated with being a victim—which is listed below in the victim checklist.

Victim Checklist

1. Constant complaining.
2. Resisting solutions and sound advice.
3. Lacking boundaries.
4. A sense of being "done wrong" all the time.
5. A fear of speaking up because someone might disagree.
6. Always borrowing money.
7. Relying on parents, even in adulthood.
8. Having unrealistic expectations from others.
9. Blaming, negativity, and excuse making.
10. Saying, "I didn't have a choice."

When You Are the Victim

What about those times when you, the leader, fall into the victim role? Believe it or not, it happens; we are all human. Don't beat yourself up or fall into denial, because awareness is the key here. You can identify your own portrayal of the victim role by noticing how and when you start to feel hopeless, as though there are no choices. The victim always feels stuck in the land of no choices, and will always—and I mean always—resist a possible solution. If you feel torn, that is an indicator that you have an integrity gap.

Responsibility is the way out of victimhood. However, you cannot choose responsibly until you recognize that you actually have choices. We often resist identifying these choices because, most of the time, the choices require us to change or to be bold. You may discover, for example, than you have to alter your demeanor from being somewhat timid to being a little more assertive. Or you may have to speak up more often rather than silently agreeing most of the time. On the other hand, you may have to tone it down a bit, or see other people's point of view more often. The bold move may include an uncomfortable conversation that should have happened two years ago, or it might mean gathering the troops, reviewing your policies, and setting a real boundary to stick to. If this sounds scary, that's actually an indicator that you are on the right track. If you feel righteous anger, then it's a sign you may be about to shift from victim to persecutor—the most dangerous place on the Triangle.

Role Reversals

Beware of the anger that often initially erupts when you finally recognize you have had enough—when you are sick and tired of your staff taking advantage, or when someone above you doesn't respect your ideas. Your anger is an indicator that you are about ready to switch roles. Role reversal occurs when the victim feels powerless and needs to use anger, power struggles, or similar types of manipulation to control the situation. It also happens when the rescuer is angry, or tired of helping the victims of the world only to feel angry and victimized for getting nothing in return.

It's easy to fall into the persecutor role once you have gotten comfortable in a relationship. Just look back at the times you have snapped at your spouse or rolled your eyes at your mother because you knew you would be forgiven.

Persecution also appears when you have helped a person time and time again, but feel as if you've gotten nothing in return. You've had enough, and you finally let her have it.

The Persecutor

The persecutor is the person in the boat who beats the others with the oars instead of rowing with the team. He blames others for his outbursts and tirades instead of learning how to master his energy and take responsibility.

Much like the victim but with more force, the persecutor spends energy and time focusing on the negative—whether it is the fault of others, what should have happened, or why everyone else is wrong. Instead of finding solutions or operating as a team member, the persecutor thinks of ways to make his point, how to get revenge and even keeps score in a sense.

The persecutor fails to see that he loses power by letting circumstances or other people pull his strings. He often has the potential to be an extremely high achiever—if he can learn to leave the role behind. The extra energy that has been used on negativity and manipulation could be harnessed to achieve greatness.

The goal when dealing with the persecutor is to convert his anger to positive action that can help him move ahead, instead of fueling the fire of his rage.

How to Identify the Persecutor at Work

The persecutor often plays the part of tattletale and trouble-maker as well. However, you may not recognize this tendency—even though all the other employees do. Because the persecutor has such an intense need to be right, she feels justified in helping the boss by looking for others' faults and mistakes. The boss appreciates this inside information, and thus sees the persecutor as a conscientious employee.

In addition, the persecutor is often extremely competent. He or she knows how to shine when the boss is around, meets the quota, and gets the job done—often at the expense of others. He or she is often the star performer—great at sales, quick and productive, and full of charismatic talent. In fact, the persecutor's ability to get things done is what makes it easier for the boss to overlook the drama he or she causes. The persecutor can be extremely hard on her own imperfections as well, which is why she works so diligently to highlight others' flaws: It keeps her from looking in the mirror and recognizing her own.

The problem here is that a lawsuit always starts out as a complaint that has gone unaddressed. Most of the time, even if the other employees point out the problem, someone in a higher position protects the persecutor—either out of seniority, a soft heart, or just plain denial.

I once worked as a consultant to a doctor's office that employed a very visible persecutor. Though I was concerned, she got away with murder because the doctor thought she was the star employee. She constantly talked trash about the other staff members—to me, the consultant! She was always right and could always find mistakes made by others.

I have also done my share of phone consulting where I encountered a very visible persecutor who bullied everyone in the office but where the manager was too afraid to talk to the partner about the problem for fear of losing her own job. As I said before, when you begin to recognize the patterns and your choices, you will be called to move boldly or to change something—and it likely will not be comfortable.

How to Eliminate Persecuting Behavior

Never let employees come to you tattling about other employees while requesting that you keep it a secret. This is the persecutor's favorite game, because she knows that you, the boss, will perceive it as helping. When Jane comes to you and says, "Charles is unhappy about the schedule, and I thought you should know," your response should be to tell Jane that Charles needs to come to you himself. You can then invite Jane to go fetch Charles. This will stop the game playing. Make it a rule (again unless it's life-threatening or an emergency) that each person must represent himself or herself, and not rescue others.

In addition, when someone has a gripe with someone else, she should be willing to speak to that person, perhaps in your presence if necessary so you can mediate. The conversation's intention should always be to repair the relationship or solve the problem. Most of the time, the natural intention is instead to get someone else in trouble.

When the Persecutor Is the Owner or Partner

Most bosses who are persecutors have a blind spot and fail to recognize their persecuting tendencies—a surefire way to lose employees. The number one reason people leave their jobs is due to poor supervisor skills and attitudes. Yelling, screaming, blaming, and verbal abuse pave a guaranteed path to eradicating employee loyalty. The persecutor is often the business owner or the managing partner—and there will usually be a high turnover if this is the case. The persecutor comes from the indignant belief that "I am in charge," "I am right and you are wrong," or "I am competent and you are clueless." The persecutor uses her power ineffectively and rationalizes her rude behavior with excuses like "That's just the way I am" or "You are getting paid; that should be enough for you."

The persecutor feels right about his perceptions and is prepared for debate. He tries to win through force—whether that is through intimidation tactics such as yelling and screaming, strict enforcement of the rules, or by punishing or dominating his underlings.

The reality, however, is that you won't receive employee loyalty if you are beating your team with the oars. You may get compliance—but just until they can find employment elsewhere. You surely won't get any level of commitment.

My advice: don't work for someone who justifies consistent persecuting behavior. Life is short. There are other jobs; it simply isn't worth it. The checklist below gives you an overview of how to identify persecutor behaviors and mind-sets.

Persecutor Checklist

1. The need to win every argument.

2. Feeling right most of the time, claiming that they can "prove it."

3. Believing that others don't see their own faults.

4. Being blunt even if feelings are hurt.

5. Perceived by others to be unapproachable.

6. Making fun of others.

7. Sarcastic and disrespectful.

8. Hitting below the belt.

9. Having consistently angry outbursts.

10. Engaging in eye rolling and other forms of discounting.

When You Are the Persecutor

The persecutor is perhaps the most interesting role, because while it's fairly easy to identify in someone else, it's difficult for people to see it in themselves. That is because you only see your own point of view when you persecute; you have analyzed the situation upside-down, backward and forward, and have found yourself to be right in every circumstance. Of course, this is also true for the victim and the rescuer.

I found myself that the more I studied the persecutor role, the more I identified with it. I have been guilty of cutting off people midsentence, using anger to get my way, or rolling my eyes in disagreement. This, again, is where clarity comes in. When you figure out what your values are and catch yourself engaging in behaviors that indicate an integrity gap, you clean the situation up quickly instead of creating more relationship drama or justifying rude behavior. Remember the goal of "no complaints, no excuses, and no regrets"? I could definitely excuse the behavior by saying "I'm just playing"; but the reality is that you will have regrets any time you go against your values. I am now crystal clear about how I want to show up in the world—and while there is always room for growth, there is no room for excuses about bad behavior.

Getting Off the Triangle

The only way off the Triangle is by accepting responsibility and adopting the mind-set of becoming a creator. Stepping off the Triangle is a process; you never will be completely drama free. The saying "You teach what you need to learn" applies here; if you teach these things to your staff, they'll become further embedded in your words and actions.

Remember this: The journey is in the gap. Life is about growth and learning from mistakes; so don't start beating yourself with the oars. That is a game of solitary drama.

Awareness

When it comes to escaping the Triangle, willingness is the key, awareness is the doorknob, and responsibility is the door. Let's turn that knob and increase the awareness before we walk through the door.

Your thoughts and emotions are clues that tell you that you are either already on the Triangle or about to shift a role. As you read the following paragraphs, become aware of distinction between "thought" and "feeling" clues. In the third principle, "Tell Yourself the Truth," we talked about how combining thought and feeling creates a story. Now we'll break this principle down a bit to see how it relates to you in real life.

Notice How You Think and Feel

If someone in your life is persecuting you or taking advantage of your good nature, then it stands to reason that you must be unconsciously playing the victim role. The answer is not to try to change her; it is to look inward and change your own patterns first.

Notice how you think and how you feel when you have enabled someone to become dependent upon your expertise, support, or competency. Are you drained because your efforts have gone unrewarded? These kinds of thoughts will lead to resentment—which is a warning sign that your persecutor is about to erupt. Beware of justifying your anger and resentment—that is a thought clue and merely a way to prove you are right. It's another form of excuse-making or getting others to agree with the rightness of your position. Even if you believe you are justified in the resentment, it doesn't warrant persecuting someone else. Remember, you don't want to create an excuse that leads to regret.

What are you thinking when you have the desire to point out all that you have done for others—all the sacrifices that were made? Are you trying to manipulate them into guilt? Do you think to yourself, "I have been taken advantage of, and now I'm going to let them know about it?" What feeling resonates with you? Are you judging them for not being who you wish they would be? Listen to your language, and see if there is any inherent blame or indication that you have been treated unfairly. All of these thoughts and feelings imply that you have been rescuing or feeling victimized, and are about to persecute.

Once you are clear, you come to realize that simply asking for what you want or setting appropriate boundaries will eliminate drama most of the time. When you believe others are capable and responsible, you will not feel the strong urge to rescue, only to regret wasting your energy on one who is not willing to take responsibility.

When you are confident that you are responsible for the contents of your life, you cannot continue being the victim for long. No one can persecute you if you remain conscious and refuse to jump on the Triangle with her. If you refuse to engage, the game comes to an end.

The Fourth Position

Dr. Stephen Karpman makes the claim that if you play one role, you are playing them all. Managers or business owners frequently know and even admit that drama is present in their workplaces. They understand that their employees are on the Triangle, but don't realize that they—the bosses—are right there next to them. If this is you, then you must know that there is a fourth position, in the middle—and it is called *denial*. This fourth position is my addition to Dr. Karpman's model to illustrate how one may be participating on the Drama Triangle but be unaware of any involvement. Denial is the drug of choice for many of us when we face difficult choices. If you recall, denial is also part of the Johari Window. It's the section in which you have a blind spot of which others—but not you—are aware, or the subconscious part that neither you nor others know about.

As a leader, you are required to be open to and see the reality of the situation—and you are required to bring your staff out of denial on a regular basis. If you are letting substandard performance, bickering, backstabbing, and other forms of drama erupt in your business, I can promise you that someone is in denial. You may justify this person's behavior because your company is going through a big change, or you may procrastinate about confronting unwanted behavior to light because you dread the conflict. However, the longer you let it go on, the uglier it is going to get. You can't escape the responsibility before you. You must constantly balance the task of motivating and leading with bringing your people out of denial.

As I said before, awakening from the drug of denial can be painful. When you shed light on another person's incompetence, rude behavior, or pattern of which they were unaware, they will become defensive. Think of how you feel when someone says "Can I give you some feedback?" This type of approach almost always feels threatening—even when the intentions are good. Your staff member may feel attacked or belittled, so make sure you approach these issues with kid gloves. I suggest that you observe these two rules:

1. Never catch anyone off guard.
2. Always correct in private and do it in a positive, team-oriented approach, with the intention of bringing out the employee's best.

Develop Other Leaders

If you sideswipe others with an observation or with feedback, they are going to land immediately on the victim point, or have a meltdown and land on the persecutor position. Establishing a self-improvement program can help with this tremendously, especially when you create the parameters for instituting a self-directed professional growth program. I believe one of the highest callings a leader can have is to develop other leaders. Through development, even those who do not have an official title can develop leadership skills.

Let's take a real workplace scenario that I received from an office manager who wants to help her receptionist, Madelyn, become more productive.

> I am the office manager for a multiphysician medical office. I supervise four full-time employees and two part-time employees. Madelyn, our receptionist, has a lot of drama and shares her personal stories—something that often disrupts our productivity. Last week, her car blew a flat tire, and the week before that, her adult son moved in with her because he went bankrupt. It is a challenge to keep her on task and focused. She tends to wander the office and socialize, and is also a type of mother hen, making sure the physicians have snacks or even going so far as to bring in extra servings of her lunch to share with the doctors. The doctors feel sorry for her because she is

overweight, has some health problems, and tends to put herself last.

I have spoken to Madelyn regarding staying on task; she usually does better for awhile, but then it drops off again. It is hard to set parameters for her to meet as the office flow can change from day to day depending on the phone and patient flow. How do you handle a personality like this, and keep her on task and in line?

As you can see, Madelyn has good traits. She gets along with others, and she is thoughtful. However, she wastes time on gossip and getting sympathy for her victim stories.

My advice to this particular person: institute a self-improvement program and select two superior performers and your problem employee. This way, there will be no red flags, and your growth program will be positioned as an experimental pilot program. You can tell everyone that you will randomly select three people to test pilot.

Second, list general criteria for the areas you want to measure—perhaps five or six—and then leave two or three growth areas open for them to determine. This gives you a measure of control while also offering the excitement of autonomy and choice. You help the participants come up with a plan of action and deadlines and a way to know if they got from point A to point B as they progress through their development program. Though it may sound complicated at first, this kind of program can be incredibly easy to institute and run. It takes a bit of planning and some time on your part to keep your employees accountable—perhaps with short, weekly meetings—but it will provide some much-needed direction.

Block out time on your schedule for one-on-one and accountability coaching sessions. Yes, this will take some effort; but in the long run, this pilot could help you keep everyone rowing together and could create lots of fun in celebrating everyone's growth.

If you have a problem that is so serious as to need to implement discipline, institute the proper support for recovery, and again, make sure there are no surprises. Your people should not be shocked to receive feedback about how they have been performing for the last three years, nor should you use your frustration to scare them with information about how everyone else perceives their performance. Be aware of your own attitude before correcting anyone else. If it feels a little like revenge, wait until you are more neutral and can share just the facts. Otherwise, your own lack of clarity for your intention can keep you trapped in the fog of drama. The way to avoid drama is to catch the problem early instead of letting it fester.

Teach the Principles in Your Workplace

I recommend teaching the concepts of the Drama Triangle to your employees in a staff-development meeting. Doing so will increase company-wide awareness and promote healthy workplace relationships. You can have some fun with these concepts, and share with each other how they play out in your personal lives. That exercise alone will create a sense of camaraderie while your staff learns valuable principles. In fact, research shows that creating teams has as much to do with camaraderie as it does with core competencies (Sirota et al. 2006). You certainly don't have to do an all-day retreat on the ropes course; just use a few simple programs to enhance solidarity between workers.

Also, make sure that you facilitate discussion instead of lecturing. You want your employees to talk about their lives, so make it fun and don't correct or criticize if they don't understand the concepts immediately. Plant the seed now; you can start referring to the concepts later as you create a drama-free workplace.

Questions to Answer

1. What is my default pattern under stress?
2. How can I empower my staff to eliminate victim behaviors?

3. What could we do to improve workplace relationships?
4. In what way could I teach my staff to see things differently?

Learning Points

- All drama has a relationship component.
- Relationship is really how you think about someone or something.
- The primary workplace relationship exists between boss and employee.
- When you see others differently, you promote their growth.
- We treat people according to how we view them.
- The Drama Triangle is a tool to help you identify drama.
- To exit the Triangle, you must recognize choice and become responsible.
- Willingness is the key, awareness is the doorknob, and responsibility is the door.
- Notice the thought and feeling clues to increase awareness.

Chapter 6

Master Your Energy

I am extraordinarily patient,
provided I get my own way in the end.
—Margaret Thatcher

All drama has three common elements: A lack of clarity, a relationship component, and an energetic component. We have already talked about clarity and relationship; this chapter is about the energetic component.

Speaker and *The Energy Bus: 10 Rules to Fuel Your Life, Work, and Team with Positive Energy* author Jon Gordon states, "No one goes through life untested, and the answer to these tests is positive energy—not the rah-rah, cheering kind of positive energy, although there certainly is a time and place for that as well. But rather . . . the optimism, trust, enthusiasm, love, purpose, joy, passion, and spirit to live, work, and perform at a higher level; to build and lead successful teams; to overcome adversity in life and at work; to share contagious energy with employees, colleagues, and customers; to bring out the best in others and in yourself; and to overcome all the negative people (whom I call energy vampires) and negative situations that threaten to sabotage your health, family, team, and success." (Gordon 2007, front flap)

The premise of "Master Your Energy" is this: Everything in the universe is made up of energy, and all energy systems work together. Therefore, the leader who understands how to master energy can help bring out the best in others. In turn, this will help to eliminate much of the complaining and excuses—not to mention turnover, burnout, and power struggles.

I believe that the cause behind many illnesses is an inability to comprehend energy mastery. Working harder with less contributes to more workplace drama due to misunderstanding, and the perception of lack, limitation, and fewer resources to handle the workload.

Energy mastery works from this premise: Since everything in the universe has energy, productivity and well-being are directly related to mastering energy. Mastering energy occurs when we create boundaries, have our needs met, and develop systems to help maximize and leverage time. The better you are at mastering your energy, the higher your personal effectiveness—and the more positive the impact you have on others.

Being in charge of your emotional, mental, spiritual, environmental, and physical energy can make you a very positive role model. I love the saying, "You can't change the world when you have trouble finding your car keys." As *The Power of Full Engagement* authors Jim Loehr and Tony Schwartz state in their book: "The more we take responsibility for the energy we bring to the world, the more empowered and productive we become. The more we blame others or external circumstances, the more negative and compromised our energy is likely to be" (Loehr and Schwartz 2003, 5).

Think of it this way: Energy is power, and we all lose power in various ways. Some of us do not get enough rest, while others let their mind wander endlessly over problems. This chapter will explain how to master your energy so that you can become more empowered and productive.

The Five Kinds of Energy

The five kinds of energy are physical, mental, emotional, spiritual, and environmental. All of these work together and impact one another. For example, everyone knows how easy it is to have an emotional outburst (or excess emotional energy) when you're overly tired (lacking physical energy).

So often we start out on a big mission with only a half tank of gas. I'm amazed by the stories we are all buying into about how it's possible to operate at full capacity without a full tank of gas or the proper tools and resources to effectively do the job.

I recently heard Mike Fabrizio, a healthcare management consultant for Medical Group Management Association, speak at a conference in Kansas City. According to Fabrizio's presentation, you cannot give your employees any more than 10 percent more workload without increasing resources. However, companies frequently downsize, double the workload, and expect the same amount of productivity. To add to the problem, employees are afraid to tell their bosses that meeting these requirements is impossible for fear that their job might be next to go. So the lie continues, and everyone is frustrated. Denial and withholding is never a good method of promoting productivity or teamwork; remember the chapter on telling yourself the truth? This is a real life example of the corporate myths we accept as true.

When your team is overworked or overwhelmed, their boat is leaking—and it will show up as backstabbing, complaining, bickering, and excuse-making.

It takes effort and time to master your energy, but in the end, you actually save time and enjoy the journey so much more. It requires that you slow down to do your mental, emotional, and spiritual work, and see this practice as a time management and productivity tool.

Most of the time, however, we do just the opposite and spiral into drama. Instead of using our emotions to let us know that we need to take a break, slow down, or process more information, we let our emotions throw us into sarcasm, outbursts, pouting, and office drama. So we jump in the boat without first loading it with the necessary supplies to make the journey easy.

The old adage that instructs professionals to leave their personal life at home isn't completely realistic nowadays. Even though there are necessary and appropriate boundaries between these two areas of your life, the fact is that human beings are not robots. Drama at home tends to find its way into your performance at work, and your problems on the job will impact your home relationships. That is why learning to master your energy is one of the best management tools you will ever learn.

Let's look at each type of energy separately, identify areas in your workplace where you may be losing energy, and determine what you can do about it.

Master Physical Energy

You live in a physical body that needs oxygen, nutrition, and rest to function. Most of us work too hard without adequate recovery time. We skip breaks, work through lunch, and make promises to get our exercise when we get caught up. But the fact is, you will never catch up. Working harder with fewer resources only contributes to more workplace drama and storytelling, as well as accidents due to exhaustion. In fact, According to the National Academy of Sciences' web site, medical errors (many of which are caused by fatigue among doctors) account for nearly 100,000 deaths a year—more than motor vehicle accidents, breast cancer, and AIDS combined.

Some symptoms of poor physical energy management are inadequate concentration, low energy, long hours with no breaks, and rude or harsh behavior. Speaker and *A Kick in the Attitude: An Energizing Approach to Recharge Your Team, Work, and Life* author Sam Glenn recommends that you recharge your "attitude batteries" regularly. He mentions that there are four main attitude vultures that can trigger a negative outlook: stress, fatigue, hunger, and negative influences. He recommends proactively treating your attitude because, as he states in his book, "It is easier to maintain a good attitude than it is to try to fix or overhaul a bad one" (Glenn 2010, 32–33).

Require Rejuvenation

Make it a requirement for your employees to engage in acts of rejuvenation to keep their attitudes positive and negativity at bay. While instituting periods of rest may violate your instincts or corporate culture, you need to see the truth: The body requires rest and rejuvenation every 60 to 90 minutes. Believe me when I say that it is possible to provide you and your staff with brief, intermittent breaks. Just stretching for five minutes or going outside to take a breath of fresh air or drink a big glass of water will decrease the likelihood of errors and increase productivity.

For example: A colleague of mine went to work for an open-source software company, Red Hat—which various independent business publications consistently rate as one of the top 100 technology companies to work for—and exclaimed at how they offer employee incentives and perks such as a room filled with free snacks, a TV to watch sports on during breaks, and access to a quality gym facility. This both rewards employees and indirectly encourages them to take breaks.

If this idea bothers you, I suggest that you examine your relationship with work, who you think you are, and who you think your employees are. This resistance may denote more of a relationship problem than an energy management problem. If you view your employees as cogs in a wheel, even allowing them a break is not going to solve your productivity problems. If that is the case, your drama is related to your relationship with others, and how you see yourself and your workplace. If unaddressed, this issue will leak out in other ways—I guarantee it.

Here is a challenging question: Are you stuck on the Triangle with a need to be right about your beliefs as they pertain to energy management? Your employees probably also want to be right about theirs. This need keeps everyone participating on the Drama Triangle. What is so fascinating is that despite our constant desire to be right, these beliefs really do not serve us very well.

I once worked with a group of women within a planning and zoning division who believed they could not take breaks. They spent a lot of time trying to convince me of the restrictions that had been placed upon them. When I finally listened long enough to gain their trust, they were able to get out of denial and consider other options.

Their company provided a planning session during which we brainstormed a way for them to relieve each other for five minutes each. It was amazing how much their morale improved when we implemented this system. Simply knowing they would be able to escape—for even five minutes—from the intense customer complaint desk and the heavy demands of their technical jobs enabled them to pitch in and help each other even more and experience a sense of freedom from the daily grind.

It falls under state laws for many hourly employees to take 15-minute breaks for every four hours of work. Those who work at fast food companies, for example, are required to utilize their breaks. Why is it that when we become salaried or move up the corporate ladder, we tend to think that breaks are not important? There is a reason why these breaks were created, after all; we don't need them less simply because we have more to do.

Do not buy into the myth that there is no opportunity for relief. Unless you are in an emergency situation or faced with an unusual circumstance that requires everyone to sacrifice for the common good, you can take and benefit from breaks. In fact, skipping breaks should be the exception, instead of the rule. To that end—do not reward the person who never takes a break and eats lunch at her desk. This just creates a platform for comparison and drama. Instead, insist that your staff take care of their physical needs with the expectation that small periods of rejuvenation will increase productivity, decrease mistakes, and heighten morale.

Master Your Mental Energy

Wouldn't it feel great to wake up every day alive with enthusiasm and positivity, quick on your feet, creative, and confident? Mastering your mental energy can help you achieve this outcome. In fact, you might even improve your sales record, as studies have linked positive thinking with the ability to sell.

The ability to think creatively is fast becoming one of the most sought-after skills in the business world. The left hemisphere and the right hemisphere of the brain have different functions. The right side, often associated with creativity, sees the big picture, has the capacity to "connect the dots," and sometimes receives intuitive impulses. The left brain, in contrast, works in a more logical sequence.

Remaining in a mental state of always trying to figure it out is exhausting and hampers productivity. Learning how to use both sides of the brain is what mental mastery is all about. This process, called *oscillation*, involves expending energy and subsequently recovering. When you are always in a mental state of figuring it out—or, on the other side of the spectrum, are always creating—you become exhausted. Your conscious mental processes take place in your frontal cortex. Since there is only so much energy in a given day, you must learn how to master your mental energy. I highly recommend reading the book *Your Brain at Work*, by David Rock, if you want to become more mentally effective. One significant way to do this is to make it easy on yourself by either automating as much as you can or developing processes and procedures.

How Processes and Procedures Save Energy

I was constantly surrounded by processes and procedures when I worked in a factory; however, I didn't fully appreciate them until I applied the same rules to my business and personal life.

It is easy for small businesses to fall into the trap of shooting from the hip or changing the rules to suit your whims. As you grow, however, these freedoms eventually become the bars that bind you. You begin to lose your rhythm and start getting behind because of too many choices and the tendency to be disorganized, which therefore requires you to constantly recreate the wheel. If you are allowing for too much creativity without good processes and procedures, I can guarantee you that some considerable drama is coming.

When you understand the power of rhythm, you can use it to motivate your team. For example, establishing a system or a standard operating procedure will help to conserve energy. In other words, once you make a decision on how things are to be done, you no longer have to make this decision again. Then when a misunderstanding occurs, you have a documented process prepared to handle it—like an employee handbook to refer to. Everyone understands the rules; they are not changed unless there is good reason. And should a good reason occur, all leaders and decision makers communicate and enforce those changes.

Create a standard operating procedure manual as a way to preserve and replicate the processes that work. The first step is to document every step you follow in a given project. For example, you might have Sandra document each step that it takes to complete the tasks her job require. This lays the foundation for growth. Then, if you want to promote Sandra, you'll have a documented training manual to which you can refer and which will allow Sandra to train her replacement. In addition, you now have a document of what Sandra's job requires, and the steps involved to carry it to fruition in case Sandra should quit or decide that she is indispensible. In other words, you have the power—not Sandra.

You may at some time decide to revise or tweak your system as new advancements in technology or other changes emerge. However, standard operating procedures—as well as an employee handbook—remove much of the mental stress of having to always figure it out.

This is common knowledge for anyone leading a team in corporate America or working in a highly regulated private practice. However, you still might be missing pieces where you could create rules, standards, or other processes that would eliminate much of the drama that is slowing you down. On the other hand, if there is no room for creativity, problem-solving, and taking responsibility, you are going to have some very bored employees who will probably search for places to work that allow them to use their talents.

However, if you can find a way to encourage creative problem solving within standard procedures—and you reward employees for increasing the profitability—you are going to have a stimulated and engaged staff. Another way to add miles to your mental capacity is through understanding how to set effective boundaries.

Setting Boundaries

I'm going to keep a promise that I made to you in an earlier chapter when I claimed that enforcing rules helps to eliminate drama. This is the ability to have a very strong no and stick to it.

One of the biggest energy-wasters in many businesses is a lack of boundaries. For all the positive hype around phrases like "no boundaries" and "no limits"—that glorify the opportunity to engage in everything under the sun as if we were skillfully skiing off cliffs—the case has already been made that too many choices can have you drowning in the sea of opportunity. Therefore, boundaries—just like discipline—can actually be more freeing than restraining.

There are a couple of definitions for "boundary," one of which is *any line or thing marking a limit; bound; border*. So, your policies and rules are types of boundaries. However, I have another definition that I believe is more inspiring: *a boundary is a frame around your choices*. Take, for example, the idea of a manager who has an open-door policy with his employees. This is not really a boundary; rather, it's an example of too many choices with no limits. This policy often encourages tattletales, brown-nosing, and drama of all sorts, and takes up valuable time that the manager could spend on planning, customer relations, and managing the business. Instead, because the manager wants to be liked, his door remains open—and in walks Sally, ready to take advantage. Sally is mad at Joe, who left her a mess for the third time, and wants you to fix it. Next is Rob, who tells you that Alice doesn't like the new schedule, but asks you to please not tell Alice that we had this conversation. Then comes Rita, who is there to tell you that she feels like Rob gets preferential treatment.

My advice: Set a boundary. Here is how it works. You tell your staff that the open-door policy is changing. Now, the door is only open on Tuesdays and Thursdays between two and four o'clock (or whatever time frame works for your business). You also create boundaries about how you want to be approached. You train your employees to set an appointment, and come to you with an agenda that includes the following: the problem, how the problem impacts productivity or teamwork, ideas for solving the problem, and choices for handling it personally. Now you have eliminated all the interruptions and your employees will start thinking like problem-solvers instead of complainers.

What do you do in those times when Sally rushes in on Monday morning at 11 o'clock? You say, "Sally, I want to help you. Let's set an appointment for Tuesday at two. Don't forget to have this paper filled out." Then you'll hand her a form with a simple line-by-line list covering the points:

- The problem.
- How this problem impacts productivity, teamwork, or customer service.
- Ideas for solving the problem.
- Choices for handling it.

If Sally comes to you without using the proper format, you can counsel her the first time. If she says, "There are no choices," tell her to reschedule for Thursday and come back with at least one idea. You have to quit allowing victim behavior.

Proper boundaries conserve energy and enhance your personal effectiveness. To promote responsible behavior with those you lead, learn how to recognize choice in the midst of any crisis.

The same principles of setting boundaries apply in your personal life. For example, this might mean not allowing telephone or electronic interruptions after 8 PM. Wouldn't that be freeing to know that you have free time to enjoy with your family, and that even though work is waiting and the iPhone is available, you have made a conscious decision that your late evenings belong to you? This example may not be appropriate for every individual—but you get the idea.

Master Emotional Energy

An emotion is a mental and physiological state associated with a wide variety of feelings, thoughts, and behaviors. The word emotion actually means "disturbance." My favorite definition of emotion comes from Eckhart Tolle in *The Power of Now: A Guide to Spiritual Enlightenment*: "An emotion is the body's response to the mind" (Tolle 2004, 25).

When you hear the word "emotion," you probably think of anger, fear, sadness, joy, excitement. Symptoms of poor emotional energy management are anger, resentment, feeling competitive, jealousy, ongoing sadness, depression, criticism of others, gossip, negativity, and pessimism.

An emotion can be triggered by a thought, or can emerge due to physiological responses, such as hormone imbalance or chemical changes within the body. It's important to remember that the body functions as a system wherein everything is connected. For example, emotions that arise out of threat, fear, and frustration are toxic and release *cortisol*, or stress hormones—and even the mere act of recalling an angry experience for as long as five minutes can suppress the immune system for up to six hours. It's clear to see how the mind and body are connected. The more we know about how they work together, the better choices we can make regarding our personal health and thus our leadership.

Emotions play such a vital role in individual health and team cohesiveness. When you understand the impact and start challenging your staff to master their emotions, you create a highly productive and impactful organization. Mastering your emotions on a personal level will increase your health, improve your personal effectiveness, and help you build rewarding relationships.

As I mentioned before, mastering physical energy by getting appropriate periods of rejuvenation helps everyone to master emotions as well. Emotional mastery is not a one-time event; it's a process.

Leaders carry a heavy load. How would the power to master your energy impact your ability to lead? Wouldn't it be great to be in control and feel confident to respond to a sarcastic comment with a deep breath and question of clarification, instead of retorting with sarcasm? Suppose a client, colleague, or patient has some negative feedback. Wouldn't it be great if you could see this criticism as information for your benefit instead of something to take personally? Wouldn't you prefer to stand firm in saying no without being angry when someone tried to manipulate you?

This is what life will be like when you master your emotions. You will no longer be controlled by an unconscious mind pattern, but instead you will be able to guide your own actions in response to the feedback you receive from life. This is what emotional mastery is all about.

We have already talked at length about the Drama Triangle, and we have emphasized the idea that drama hampers productivity. Next, I want to provide some tools to share with your team to promote emotional mastery.

The first tip—after you make a commitment to regular rejuvenation to support physical energy mastery—is *to live in the zone*.

Living in the Zone

Part of what drains energy emotionally and mentally is living too far into the future and/or too far in the past. Living in the past usually makes you feel guilty or regretful about what could have been. An example of this might be the resentment you feel about an employee who caused you trouble when you merged offices. The employee may be cooperating now, but due to your history and a residual grudge, there is still a lot of relationship tension.

You spend too much time and energy looking for faults, withholding, and resisting your commitment to develop this employee.

Living too far into the future will have you sick with anxiety about what could happen if you mess up or things don't go as planned. You either look forward with anxiety and worry, or anticipate that the future will bring the salvation from all your problems.

When you live too much in the past or future, you negate the only real power you have—that which you hold in the present moment. You may believe that when the new software gets installed, then things will become more organized. When you move into the new building, everyone will start working together more efficiently.

However, the future never really offers salvation. You get the new software, and there is a learning curve; right when you become accustomed to using it, a new version comes out. You move into the new building, but the newness wears off soon enough. There is always disappointment when we see the future as the answer to the problem. You can only solve the problem now; but because you resist the now, you feel frustrated and overwhelmed.

One way to break this habit and focus your energy on the present is to live in the zone. Think of this as a number line, with negative 10 to the left and positive 10 to the right. In the middle is zero, which represents the present moment. You want to live—and teach your staff to live—between negative 2 and positive 2. At negative 2, you are learning from the past; at positive two, you are merely glancing ahead at what needs to be done. If you as the leader are living in the zone, you are always learning, glancing, and using your present moment appropriately (see Figure 6.1).

This tool can get you back on track very quickly when you are wasting precious time and energy on regrets or worry.

The second method will show you how to create an energetic starting place. In other words, you can learn to set your

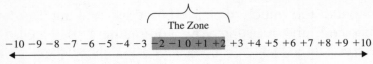

Figure 6.1   The Zone

focus in advance—before any potentially stressful activity, discussion, or interaction.

Create an Energetic Starting Place

Mastering your energy emotionally means knowing where you are starting from, versus jumping in blindly to hurriedly get going. In other words, you have an emotional and mental starting place for every task, conversation, and activity—whether you are delivering a speech, reprimanding an employee, asking for a raise, or hosting a company picnic.

We often deceive ourselves about our starting points; it isn't easy to admit that you feel desperate, angry, frustrated, and worried. The key is to become conscious of your energetic state and your intention before you start any task. When you aren't aware of where you are coming from, a discussion with an employee turns into a power struggle, a small complaint can send you into orbit, or a suggestion from the CEO has you applying for a position with the competitor.

Emotionally, spiritually, and mentally speaking, your starting point—your intention and state of mind—fundamentally determines your journey and even your final outcome.

The problem is that most of us are not aware enough of our emotional states before we begin an interaction. Have you ever surprised yourself by having a conversation that turned ugly without even realizing that you had a kernel of resentment toward the other person? Without warning, you undercut someone with your quick wit and sharp tongue. To paraphrase one of my favorite authors, Gary Zukav: "If you are not aware of your intention before an interaction, you will become aware of it afterward" (Zukav and Francis 2003, 43). Your final response to any interaction tells you where you were really starting from and what your real intention was—no matter what you initially thought.

Master Your Spiritual Energy

Spiritual energy is about values and purpose. My spiritual energy changed when I got perfectly clear that I was committed to improving communication and relationships everywhere. This new mind-set—based on solid character-based values—impacted every decision and interaction in my business.

When consultants help businesses with their mission and vision, what they are really doing is helping you align your purpose to your prosperity. That's all it is. It doesn't have to be difficult. Just figure out your role and your objectives, and then see if these align with what you say and how you act—or if you're stuck in the integrity gap that we discussed earlier.

Tell yourself the truth. What are you really committed to? What drives you internally? How can you get your employees to tie their individual purposes to your company mission and vision? If it does not align in some way, you may get compliance—but not commitment. If you can help build your staff's talents and use their skills and intellect, then you're on the right path.

One way we drain ourselves in this area is by biting off more than we can chew. As a leader, you can manage this problem by making sure power is evenly distributed. This is done by balancing choice with responsibility.

Balance Choice and Responsibility

You may find when you work with high achievers that they tend to be interested in gaining more power through promotions, executive titles, and bigger opportunities. All of us have witnessed a dramatic increase in title and opportunity, only to see a drastic failure as a result. I believe that this is a sort of spiritual crisis, wherein the person who gained the additional opportunity was not ready emotionally, mentally, and most of all, spiritually. Their values were not clear enough, or the opportunity was too big and offered too many temptations for them to hold to their highest intentions. It takes a lot of internal strength to accept significant opportunities.

If choice is not balanced with responsibility—along with a commitment to personal mastery—drama is sure to follow. If we want the choice to engage in activities, we need to be willing to accept the responsibility that comes with the action. If we are unaware that we are taking on more than we can chew, the negative impact has a ripple effect on our customers.

Consider the major bank mergers that occurred during 2008 to 2010, in the midst of the foreclosure problems and the federal loan remodifications. I heard of one individual who had been in the midst of foreclosure when the initial remodification was offered. He was told by the newly merged bank to ignore the series of foreclosure and lack-of-payment notices that would continue to arrive, stating that they were due to a paperwork glitch that would get sorted out by the bank once the merger was more solidified. So, he ignored these notices, while continuing to pay his mortgage as requested.

Two years later, the bank again tried to foreclose, stating that they had never received all of the mortgage checks he'd been sending during that period. Additionally, his credit became destroyed, because the bank showed on paper that he hadn't made a loan payment in years. He called multiple times to explain the situation, got transferred, and finally ended up at the office of the bank CEO. To this date, he has not received resolution, and continues to struggle with credit issues.

Clearly, the bank took on more than it could handle in this case by merging before it had its ducks in a row to handle all the chaos and paperwork required of these remodifications. They failed to anticipate and repair a major leak in the boat. Now, they run the risk of federal investigations and class-action lawsuits.

Too Much Too Soon Equals Drama

Experiencing too many changes and making too many choices—without examining these choices' value and impact on our lives—can contribute to bad decision making as well as to unproductive and potentially threatening habits.

All of us currently experience this imbalance because choice outweighs our ability to act responsibly. We live with fewer and fewer boundaries and get increasingly more choices. It is exhausting to try and keep up with the pace.

For example, we are all addicted to the notion that technology is going to save time. However, what often occurs when we implement a new technological device or application is that a new demand emerges, and the expectation changes. Technology gives you new choices, but the problem is that most of us are drowning in the sea of choices and aren't really sure what is required to be responsible to all the new options. Or we free ourselves in one area, and with our new-found extra time we commit to yet another responsibility—leaving us with no overall gain in free time. We do not know how to let some of those choices go, or we do not yet have the skills to delegate. This leaves us feeling overwhelmed—an impact on self-esteem that does little for eliminating drama in the workplace.

The danger I see with emerging technology—and the powerful choices that all of us have—is that we aren't really equipped to handle the power we're given. Most of us have a love-hate relationship with technology. It is addictive. It's fun. It expands your mind. It lets you do more, and more things at one time. But it also has caused us to lose a sense of balance, and our obsession and addiction have created a situation where change drives us instead of us driving change.

We have yet to see the entirety of the effects of this imbalance; however, some areas of life and work have been altered by now. Already, new laws are being developed to keep people from texting while driving. This serves as just another example of how, because we are not responsible, we need new limits imposed upon us.

The more conscious choice is that we willingly see how to be responsible with the power of each new choice. One who learns how to master energy has the insight to look ahead, knowing that with each new choice a new requirement of responsibility is born.

We have become unconscious in many respects and often do not know how to balance choice and responsibility. This is vital to energy management—a concept I illustrate with the image of a teeter-totter.

The Teeter-Totter Effect

As most of us learned sometime during high school physics, a teeter-totter rests on something called a *fulcrum point*. When the teeter-totter is balanced, it's completely horizontal. When it is not, one end rests higher than the other. If you want the teeter-totter to be completely level and you have a 20-pound weight called "choice" on the right side, then you must have another 20-pound weight called "responsibility" on the left.

Why This Is Important for Leaders

If you work in an environment where there are opportunities for advancement and promotion, make sure your employees understand that with more power comes more responsibility. This makes them aware that when a promotion occurs, it is not just for the title and prestige; there are requirements that come with leadership. It's not just about being a boss over other people. Leadership requires wisdom and self-control. Too much power without responsibility is corrosive to individuals and to corporations.

On a more personal level, most of us—including your staff—are often asked to handle a schedule that's nearly impossible to manage. Because of this, we feel frustrated, angry, and overwhelmed instead of enjoying our work and feeling like we are contributing. We are out of balance. There are too many choices without sufficient boundaries, which creates frustration. We can work 24/7 and still never feel like we're doing enough.

This is what I mean when I refer to the imbalance of choice and responsibility. We are buying into the notion that there just isn't enough time, when in reality, there are just too many choices. This myth creates a leak in the boat that just gets bigger and bigger—because no one thinks there is time to pull over and plug it.

Your boat's location and the people in it with you comprise your environment. Let's look at this next, and figure out how to master the energy here.

Mastering Your Environment

Your environment either supports or drains your energy. Though I could talk about keeping the clutter at bay and staying organized here, I won't; there are many other good books out there that will guide you on cleaning out the clutter. The area I want to cover is about the people in your environment—your team. How can you keep everyone rowing together? Haven't you walked into a business where you could just feel the energy or lack of energy? Very often, your physical environment is just a symptom of the energy of the people in it. I want to share with you the importance of authentic communication and focus.

Authentic Communication

Despite the fact that communication plays such a significant role in teamwork, most of us are afraid to communicate authentically. A quote from the book *Crucial Conversations: Tools for*

Talking when Stakes Are High, by Kerry Patterson, Joseph Grenny, Ron McMillan, and Al Switzler, gives the following superb advice: "Start with heart. If you can't get yourself right, you'll have a hard time getting the dialogue right. When conversations become crucial, you'll resort to the forms of communication that you grew up with—debate, silent treatment, manipulation, and so on" (Patterson et al. 2002, 27–28). This concept builds on what I spoke about earlier: We need to see ourselves and other people differently, and avoid the tendency to see others as enemies.

As I also mentioned before, you need to create an energetic starting place. If you know your intention, you will be headed toward the island called "authentic communication" instead of the one called "I'm right, you're wrong." New research supports the notion that others can sense your emotional state and be influenced by it.

Research from HeartMath, a scientific institute that has been researching heart intelligence and stress management, claims that the heart has intelligence equal to the intelligence of the brain. HeartMath Institute claims the heart produces an electromagnetic field that can be measured up to 10 feet away by scientific measuring devices. I interpret this information in this way: People can sense your energy when your heart is in the right place. You know when you meet someone and get a feeling about this person? To quote the HeartMath web site:

"The heart is the most powerful generator of electromagnetic energy in the human body, producing the largest rhythmic electromagnetic field of any of the body's organs. The heart's electrical field is about 60 times greater in amplitude than the electrical activity generated by the brain. This field, measured in the form of an electrocardiogram (ECG), can be detected anywhere on the surface of the body. The electromagnetic signals generated by the heart have the capacity to affect others around us. Our data indicate that one person's heart signal can affect another's brainwaves, and that heart-brain synchronization can occur between two people when they interact. Finally, it appears that as individuals increase psychophysiological coherence, they become more sensitive to the subtle electromagnetic signals communicated by those around them. Taken together, these results suggest that cardioelectromagnetic communication may be a little-known source of information exchange between people, and that this exchange is influenced by our emotions."

This highlights the significance of mastering your emotions before working with a client or discussing an important issue with your staff.

We often find ourselves intimidated by someone who has a more blunt style, or is too touchy feely, or who doesn't seem quite as intelligent; therefore, we discount any contribution they might have.

I once had a client who was a company co-owner, one of two brothers who jointly ran the family business they had inherited from their father. William was the CEO and 10 years older than his brother Rodney, who had just joined the business as a partner three years earlier. Rodney was frustrated because he was bursting at the seams with new ideas that could take the company forward, but was too terrified of his older brother because he viewed William as a father figure. Besides, he reasoned, William had been running the business for seven years before Rodney ever stepped foot inside.

No matter how much encouragement and coaching I gave Rodney, he claimed to already know what William would say, and he was not even willing to risk asking for a conversation. From Rodney's perspective, William always discounted his ideas, and was very closed-minded. Perhaps William was in denial, but we could also assume that Rodney perceived himself as a victim and felt powerless. Rodney continued to feel hopeless, unfulfilled, and unhappy, even though he was a co-owner of the company and second in command.

Can you see how this scenario portrays all the traits we have talked about that could take people off of the Triangle: willingness, awareness, and responsibility? If you adopt a victim's energy, you'll project it onto the situation before you have an opportunity to solve it. But if you take on the attitude of someone who is capable of implementing change, you are more apt to be met receptively.

How to Have an Authentic Conversation

There is a communications-based program I teach that I have already mentioned several times in this book. I call it the LABOR principles, which stands for Listen, Ask for What You Want, Boundaries, Own Your Stuff, and Represent Yourself.

Once you are clear on your intention, and have cleaned up any negativity and assumptions about the other people, approach them with an open heart to listen—even if it seems difficult. As Stephen R. Covey (*7 Habits of Highly Effective People*) stated should be our Habit #5: "Seek first to understand instead of seeking to be understood" (Covey 1989, 239). This will put you in the right frame of mind.

When the person with whom you are talking offers resistance, simply acknowledge or ask a question. For example: "It seems like you are concerned. Am I reading you correctly?" This will tell you not only if you are on the right track or not, but also whether he is ready to listen to you.

Acknowledging and asking questions is a critical part of listening. A person will not be able to hear your ideas until she feels safe and understood. So, even if she interrupts or disagrees, take a breath, listen, and say, "Tell me more." Be curious, instead of being bound by your own agenda. You may even change your mind as you hear the concerns.

Once you have the other person's attention, then ask for what you want. Since you will have determined this in advance, you won't resort to negativity or defensiveness based on what you have just heard. Be clear about the outcome you want for this particular conversation. Let's say you just want to hash out some ideas, but you are afraid of an argument. Instead of saying "I don't want to argue with you," say instead "I want us to consider some ideas, then come to an agreement that works for both of us." Now you have focused on the positive.

Be ready to set some boundaries, the "B" part of LABOR. In other words, place limits and objectives on your choices: "How about we decide at least on part A of the proposal by Tuesday at noon, and if I don't hear from you, I will assume that you are in agreement with part A." Now you have a deadline, and your choice feels easy instead of overwhelming. You didn't ask him to read all 50 pages—just section A.

Boundaries are also your friend if the conversation takes a negative turn. "You know, Mike, I sense that we are both exhausted and frustrated. I'm going to take a break. When should we resume talking about this?" Remember that in order for a boundary to be real, you have to have some measure of control. A boundary only works if it is something you can uphold without relying on others to cooperate.

The next part of the LABOR principles—Own Your Stuff— means that you have to take responsibility for the part that you played in any of the drama. Starting the conversation with the "O" part can sometimes work wonders if the relationship is not in top shape.

Here's an example: "Mike, I have a confession to make. I have been avoiding bringing in this proposal to you because I was worried about your reaction. I have procrastinated, and I know this has probably put you behind." Observe how Mike responds. If you are sincere, and Mike is a moderately reason-able guy, chances are that his heart will soften—and you will have laid a foundation for more open communication.

This step is the cornerstone of the LABOR principles, because it virtually eliminates all threat and promotes coopera-tion. Even if Mike persecutes or responds rudely, asking for what you want again—"Mike, I want us to collaborate," or "Mike, I am on your side"—should do the job.

Represent Yourself is the last part of LABOR. Basically this is a reminder that no matter how you feel in the moment and despite how Mike acts, you must be completely aware that you are always representing yourself. Get clear on how you want to be perceived, then see yourself that way before you go to your meeting.

Focus Your Energy

Focus is an extremely important way to master team energy. Have you ever heard the phrase "what you focus on expands"? If you concentrate on what is not working, you get more of the same. Focusing on the negative simply breeds more negativity.

Focus is a huge part of goal setting. So often even though we have measurable goals, our focus ends up detached from what we really need to reach the goal. Maybe we focus on rowing instead of on the outcome, which is getting to the island. Canadian-based business coach and award-winning entrepreneur Cathy Demers, founder of Motivational Resources, explains this concept on her web site (magneticgoals.com) when she talks about her process of helping companies create what she calls magnetic goals.

Having taken one of Demers's goal-setting programs, I know firsthand that she teaches a technique she calls "measure what you treasure." The concept is based on the best use of a small part of your brain called the Reticular Activating System. Demers shared the following example from her company with me in a personal interview:

> "Our company's marketing team was focused on increasing web site visibility using SEO, search engine optimization. [We invested] lots of energy toward increasing hits to our web site. Then it dawned on me one day while in a meeting: what we really need is more prospects."

Demers's example emphasizes the fact that we occasionally forget why we are doing what we do, and focus on the boat instead of on the island. When that happens, our energy is wasted on the wrong things—which causes us to lose motivation.

Can You See the Difference Focus Makes?

Lots of energy will be wasted if your team is focused on the wrong goals. You might see this often in a sales organization, where the goal is to make 30 calls a day. Is that really the goal, or is that an assumption that making 30 calls a day will lead you to an outcome of 10 new clients per day? If you focus just on the calls, then you may still reach the goal of making 30 calls—but nothing guarantees that you'll have your 10 clients per day. Focusing on the right goal and measuring those results will magnetize your goals. Demers continues:

> "The marketing team reset their goal to generate qualified customer inquiries, and immediately . . . started so see all sorts of opportunities everywhere! When they turned their attention and focus to . . . the Magnetic Goal of customer inquiries, they began to see and pursue strategies that most often had little to do with web site traffic. The company's business results (revenues) improved dramatically, generating qualified customer inquiries for our sales team. We call these most important goals Magnetic Goals because they focus our thoughts, our energy, and our decision making on seeing and doing the things that will generate the business results that are most important to us."

If your team's goals are not giving you the results you're looking for, perhaps your focus needs to shift to measure what you treasure.

Manage Your Goals to Sharpen the Focus

Everything is energy—and each type of energy is a portal of sorts. Rather than looking at each component separately, realize that any one of these areas can bring about positive changes. If you require rejuvenation and get it, you will have more mental clarity. When you get your team excited about how the company goals contribute to their well being, you add gas to the tank. When you set boundaries, you create calm instead of chaos.

Questions to Answer

1. Where do I most often lose energy?
2. Where do I need to set some boundaries?
3. With whom do I need to have an authentic conversation?
4. What measures can we take to sharpen our focus?

Learning Points

◆ Good leadership requires self-mastery.
◆ Leaders set the workplace climate.
◆ Scattered energy invites chaos.
◆ You must require rejuvenation to increase productivity.
◆ Never add more than 10 percent to the workload without adding resources.
◆ You must always balance choice with responsibility.
◆ Boundaries create a frame around choice.
◆ Know your energetic starting place.
◆ Good process is good energy management.

Chapter 7

Release Resistance

The pessimist complains about the wind; the optimist expects it to change; the realist adjusts the sails.

—William A. Ward

Wouldn't it be awesome if leadership was as easy as setting reachable goals and having a few authentic conversations and everyone would be rowing together? The reality, however, is that life is not that simple. No matter how great you are as a leader, you will face what I believe to be one of the biggest roadblocks to productivity and personal effectiveness: resistance.

Leaders face resistance on a daily basis. Teams resist working together. Individuals resist change. Perhaps you even resist the most difficult parts of your job.

The core of resistance is what author Eckhart Tolle describes in *The Power of Now* as the "nonacceptance of what is" (Tolle 2004, 33). You avoid because you don't want to face whatever it is that you don't want to face. You complain because you can't deal with a certain situation, or you justify an angry outburst because you cannot accept the hand that has been dealt to you. How many times have you heard the same friend complain about her mean boss or sloppy husband? Complaining denotes an unwillingness or inability to let go of what can't be controlled, or to face and act on what can be changed.

The premise of releasing resistance is this: You cannot solve a problem until you accept the situation. When you jump into a solution before releasing resistance, you will just experience more drama. The solution only comes after you let go of your resistance.

Resistance can be identified by four main energy patterns. When these are broken, they allow the one who is resisting (you or someone else) to take full responsibility for facilitating or navigating change. Those four main energy patterns are *blame, resentment, justification,* and *judgment.* I teach a method of recognizing these patterns as you listen and observe behavior in my workshops. For now, just know that resistance is always a state of nonacceptance and an avoidance of responsibility.

Nonacceptance starts as a thought impulse such as, "I don't want to go through this (fill in the blank)." That thought triggers an emotional response such as frustration, dread, irritation, or guilt, then quickly materializes into more observable behaviors such as anger outbursts, finger pointing, blaming, as well as subtle behaviors such as avoidance and procrastination. In the end, resistance boils down to an unconscious avoidance of responsibility, which spirals into negativity, then finally into full-blown drama.

What is most difficult to accept is that resistance and your own unhappiness are not due to the unwanted situation. They creep in because of how you think about the situation. In other words, your relationship to the situation is more important than the situation itself. Remember how we discussed in Chapter 4 about relationships, and how we are always in relationship with whatever is causing our drama—a situation, person, or thing? If you want to change a situation, the easiest way is to first change how you think about the situation. If you can become conscious enough to first change your relationship to the situation, you'll avoid the trap of trying to force change through resistance.

The illusion is always that if the situation or person would change, then your problem would be solved. But all this illusion does is to create more drama—because it places the power outside of your control. Your sanity and peace of mind depend upon another person or a preferred situation. You only make resistance stronger when you attribute your drama to another person or an unwanted situation.

For example—avoiding a difficult conversation with an employee eventually leads to frustration. You believe that everything would work out if your employee would just change. You resent her for putting you in this position. She's an idiot, you tell yourself, and then you feel guilty for thinking bad thoughts. Because you are focused on the negativity, all you can see are the problems, flaws, and mistakes this employee makes on a continual basis. You dread coming to work, and your attitude impacts the rest of the team.

That is how resistance turns quickly into negative energy in the form of complaining, backstabbing, bickering, and power struggles. The underlying problem is your own resistance and inability to recognize it—and thus take responsibility for it.

You Resist Every Day

Resistance is difficult to recognize, because it is actually as natural to us as breathing. You start resisting before you ever walk through the doors of work. When you look in the mirror and see that your clothes are tight, do you avoid the scale and mentally beat yourself up? That is resistance. What is your reaction when you get stuck in traffic? Do you curse, get upset, worry about being late, blame the construction crew? The traffic is the drama, but your drama is your resistance to what is. That is what serves as the obstacle to your peace, at least momentarily— and it's how resistance is played out on a daily basis before we even enter the office.

Resistance Is a Form of Drama

I realized how often we complain one day when I was at a local festival called Cider Days. The sun was shining with not a cloud in the sky, and I was visiting the booths of pottery, jewelry, and art. That's when I noticed how hot the sun was on my head. My hair felt like it was on fire. Without much thought I heard my voice say "It's really hot."

My neighbor agreed. "That sun is really bearing down."

"Yep, there's not a cloud in the sky to give any relief," I continued.

Several times, I would go to a booth and get under the awning and feel a sense of relief, but every time I stepped out into clear view, I felt the heat of the sun. With the sensation, I felt the impulse to comment on how hot it was. My urge to complain felt like an addiction. I couldn't seem to stop myself. In fact, ask yourself (and be totally honest) if there isn't a little bit of hidden pleasure when you go on a rant and start complaining? I noticed how difficult it was to avoid the urge to get agreement about the discomfort of the sun at high noon.

Finally, a thought occurred, and it was almost as if I heard an audible voice saying, "Get in the shade or go home . . . everything else is just drama."

Resistance is always a time waster and therefore breeds more drama.

Instead of doing the one or two things you could actually do to solve the problem, serve the customer, or fix the mistake, you waste time complaining about who is wrong, what someone should have done, and what you didn't like about something or someone. If two employees who make $20 per hour visit at the water fountain complaining no more than one hour per week, or an average of 12 minutes per day per person, that equals $2,000 per year lost time due to complaining. That might not be that large a problem if you could contain the negativity to two people—but, unfortunately, negativity spreads like a virus.

Negativity Breeds Negativity

There are at least two ways that negativity creates more negativity. First, you get what you look for. Are you familiar with the notion of RAS—the reticular activating system—a structure in the brain that helps you find what you look for? Suppose, for example, that you decide to purchase a new car and choose a white Lexus SUV. Now all of the sudden, you see them everywhere. This is because you brought a white Lexus SUV into your awareness and now your RAS is helping you find what you are looking for. In other words, you have now programmed your subconscious to help you find what you are focusing on.

To that end—if you are focusing on what everyone else is doing wrong, you will find plenty of evidence to prove yourself right. Of course, being right and resisting only keeps you on the Drama Triangle; but at least nothing is ever your fault. The only problem is, you are the one experiencing the discomfort and ever-expanding drama.

The brain changes as a function of where you put your attention. Every time you vent, you grow a new brain cell for the purpose of venting, says Ellen Weber, president and CEO of MITA International Brain Based Center, in an article in *HR Magazine*, "The Brain at Work" (March 2008).

While this doesn't mean that you should ignore the negative, there is a difference between observing and complaining. When you observe that which you do not want, do so with the mind-set of quickly finding a solution or accepting what you cannot change. Continuing to focus on what is not working—and bringing others on the bandwagon—only feeds the fire of drama.

It's bad enough when the staff has drama—but it's even worse when the boss is negative. In their book *The Power of Full Engagement,* Jim Loehr and Tony Schwartz remind us of the responsibility leaders have to affect the organization's climate (Loehr and Schwartz 2003, 5). Research tells us that the number one reason employees leave companies is due to relationship problems with the boss. People leave bosses, not organizations.

Negativity Is Common

If you are the boss, try not to judge your staff too soon or beat yourself up. We are all in this together, and negativity is completely normal. People think over 60,000 thoughts per day—and more than 95 percent of those thoughts are either negative or repetitive. The brain is programmed for negativity. According to *Buddha's Brain* author Rick Hanson, the brain is like Velcro for negative experiences and like Teflon for positive ones (Hanson 2009, 41). Plus, many of us believe that complaining is a way to manipulate change in some way. But just as complaining about the heat does nothing to give you shade, negativity never solves a problem.

Why then do we participate in blaming, complaining, back-stabbing, and gossiping? We do it to lessen the pain and discomfort that taking responsibility requires of us.

The one thing that each person can take responsibility for is our frame of mind or attitude. Responsibility compels us to look at the part we played in any unwanted situations. We made assumptions. We didn't explain your expectations thoroughly. We didn't confront the problem when it was small. We didn't speak our truth. We didn't do a good job leading. Because of our reluctance to face these facts, it's often easier to beat ourselves up, complain about how inefficient our assistant is, or judge others for not having the skills we thought they had than it is to face the situation and figure out how to solve it.

Complaining only serves to anchor the boat in place, or slowly chip away at its hull until it leaks. Others will join your drama if you complain about the sun. Misery loves company. And while complaining and judging does nothing to solve your problem, it does make you feel better about yourself. If you have drama in the office, it's much easier to talk about the staff than it is to shore up your leadership skills. You can always find other managers who agree that a bunch of women working together spells drama. Criticizing them and finding allies in your negativity makes you right about how they are; however, it prevents you from opening to the possibility of transformational change through leadership.

Where there is drama in the office, there is a leak in the boat. What is your response? They should have checked out the boat maker. They should have avoided the rock. Now you have a reason why you didn't get to your island, and that reason feels better than it does to admit that you didn't delegate properly, provide training, or lead properly. You get to whine to other leaders who have the same problems and you conclude that it's just darn hard to get good help.

Does That Mean I Should Just Give Up?

Releasing resistance is not about giving up or letting out a sigh of resignation to say, "Oh well, I guess we just better accept things the way they are." Nor does it give license to a boss to tell a complaining employee, "You might as well accept it, or find another job." Releasing resistance does not mean you are not free to seek change; rather, it means that you recognize the choice to facilitate positive change, or to accept what is, or as I learned at Cider Days, to get in the shade or go home.

You cannot facilitate lasting change from negative energy. All the complaining in the world about how hot the sun is will not give you the relief you seek. Only recognizing the choice to get in the shade, buy a hat, or go home will give you the solution. But first you have to quit complaining and accept what is.

A Kick in the Attitude author Sam Glenn states in his speeches, "Don't complain about what you tolerate." If you are tolerating certain behaviors in your workplace, recognize the fact that you do have choices to ask for change, set boundaries, or when possible, remove yourself from the unpleasant situation. No matter what your choice, remember there are always consequences that follow your choices.

Choosing instead of complaining puts you back in control. If there appears to be no choice in your current situation, then you can still release any resistance you have to what is. In that state of release, you will be of sound mind to spot the opportunities.

It's absolutely necessary to release resistance and accept what is before you can do anything productive about the situation you want to change. In other words, you separate the drama (the situation) from your drama (your reaction) before you react or respond. Before you make any big change, clean your energy. Get clear about your real intention. Do not be fooled into thinking you can complain, finger point, manipulate, and argue your way into positive change—because positive change cannot come from a negative mind-set.

How to Know if You Are Resisting

Resistance is when you say, "There's a leak in the boat. I can't believe I got in this boat. Why does this always happen to me? I will find out who is responsible. Someone is going to pay for this!" Do you see the nonacceptance and time-waster that resistance is?

On the other hand, nonresistance is when you say, "There's a leak in the boat. I need to get it plugged up and figure out why it happened so it doesn't happen again." Now you have identified the problem, used your energy to figure out a solution, and are prepared to move forward. It is the difference between looking at low sales numbers and fit throwing, versus looking at low sales numbers and seeking new ideas and solutions.

Blame, Resentment, Justification, and Judgment

To review, you will see at least one of these four patterns in any type of resistance: blame, resentment, justification, and judgment. I call these *the four energy patterns of resistance*. Our culture unfortunately supports these four patterns as normal behavior. Here is an example:

I would have been on time, but the phone kept ringing. (Blame)

I didn't get a cup of coffee because you took the last one. (Resentment)

Well, everyone else gets away with it, so I thought it would be okay. (Justification)

My boss is a complete jerk. (Judgment)

Blame is common. We hear it all the time. The others are a little more difficult to recognize—so let's discuss these concepts for a moment.

You've probably heard your kids use justification as a way to avoid punishment. "Well, everyone else is doing it," they will say, trying to persuade you to see the logic of their bad choices.

My dad used to say, "If everyone else stuck their head in a toilet, would you also stick your head in a toilet?" It makes me laugh to recall this vivid, if somewhat unpolished, attempt at communicating a basic truth. We must make our decisions based on who we are, not on what everyone else is doing. Unfortunately, justification is just as common on Wall Street and Main Street as it was in my own backyard.

Resentment creeps in when you think someone else is responsible for your experience. Several years ago in a workshop, I had a woman participant who was extremely angry at the person who trained her on her job. "She didn't give me any additional learning guides to help me make a very important distinction before taking on my new role," she said.

"Did you ask her for the help while you were in the training?" I asked.

"I didn't think of it until later."

"What about asking her to give you some mentoring now?"

She hadn't thought of that either. She didn't want to bother her. Instead of asking, her default was to make up a story about it being too late or not wanting to bother someone.

Resentment frequently creeps in because we believe someone is withholding information, or because we did not take the responsibility to ask for what we really need.

Have you ever said, "He is so clueless. It's no wonder we have such a mess"? This is a way of judging someone else as inferior and promoting yourself. What is so interesting about judgment is how it totally blocks peace and prosperity. When you judge someone, you elevate yourself; you see them not as a friend or partner but rather as someone less than you. Doing this causes you to miss opportunities to learn from them and get new ideas.

Beware of how you resist when you are judging someone else, it usually means you are attacking their character. Resistance, no matter what form it takes almost always indicates avoiding responsibility. Is that how you want to represent yourself?

Victim Language Is Part of Our Culture

Our thoughts, language, and behaviors represent us in one of two ways every day—as people who are either *resistant* or *responsible*. We always have the choice to respond, but most of our thoughts and behaviors are programmed on auto-pilot, which comes across in much of our language.

Before you beat yourself with the oars, recognize the fact that victimization is part of our culture. Just listen to popular country or pop music and much of the music is based on blaming, resenting, justifying, or judging. A current example is Carrie Underwood's song about vandalizing her boyfriend's car in her song, "Before He Cheats." Carrie Underwood takes on the persona of a jilted girlfriend who slashes the tires and carves up the leather seats of her cheating boyfriend's car. In the song, she justifies her destructive behavior as a way to teach the cheating boyfriend a much needed lesson, ending the song with, "Maybe he'll think next time before he cheats."

How easy it is to justify violent behavior within ourselves as an appropriate response to how someone else has behaved. Justification helps us to avoid personal responsibility. Is it any coincidence that this song hit number one on the charts, has sold more than 3 million copies, and won the 2007 People's Choice Award for favorite country song?

Although Carrie Underwood is a brilliant artist (and I admit to liking the tune), I wonder how much we may be influenced in our work life and beyond because of what we are exposed to.

Listen for Clues

When you become a good listener, you'll not only be able to identify the patterns of resistance in popular culture and con- versations; you can use this skill to lead others. You can ask a question when you're interviewing a potential employee and listen for blame, resentment, justification, and judgment. When you try to figure out who is going to be a troublemaker, just listen to the patterns. This skill will help you hire responsible, positive, problem-solving people instead of blaming, negative, resistant people.

If you are not aware of these patterns, you too will get pulled in. I repeatedly see leaders who have the wool pulled over their eyes because there is a master manipulator in the workplace. She exerts power over a boss or executive because she has learned how to create chaos and justify her tattling, backstabbing, and other detrimental habits. Whoever is in charge tends to excuse much of her bad behavior because she's a top producer or has seniority. Whenever there is a lack of responsibility, there are usually a lot of reasons why things didn't work out or simply are the way they are. This is called *justification*.

The justification in this case might be "We wouldn't survive without her," or "Well, she has problems, but her good qualities outweigh her bad." This shows how operating within the four patterns of blame, resentment, justification, and judgment keeps everyone on the Triangle instead of rowing to the island.

Responsibility Is the Recognition of Choice

As you learn to listen for the kind of resistant language that—believe it or not—we all use, you will see a common component: No one recognizes that they have a choice. Here is a concept to memorize: Responsibility is the recognition of choice.

Turning Complainers into Problem-Solvers

As we discussed in a previous chapter, you need to teach your employees to bring an idea, partial solution, or suggestion for moving forward when they come to you with a complaint. Now, the options don't necessarily have to be the best choices, or the right ones—but simply recognizing that there are choices will enable someone to leave the victim role behind. They can then find the power to make a suggestion, accept what is, or ask for what they want in a way that benefits the whole organization.

A leader's job is to help others figure out how to work together to fulfill the group or organization's goals. In order to do this effectively, a leader must do his part to develop responsible employees. Obviously, most leaders have already done a fair amount of development on themselves; otherwise, they probably wouldn't be in this management position. The process of self-growth is an ongoing one for everyone. Quality leadership is about setting an example, developing others, and helping the staff to recognize choice.

The Wizard of Oz

One of my favorite movies as a child was the classic *The Wizard of Oz*. Dorothy's pair of ruby red slippers gave her power; but because she was not aware of it, she spent her energy and time looking outside of herself to find a way home. She met others on her journey—the Tin Man, the Scarecrow, and the Lion—all of whom were looking outside of themselves for the answers. The lesson we learn at the end of the movie is one that's all too easily forgotten: Each of these characters already had what they were seeking. They just had to look further inside themselves to find it.

Responsibility is a lot like this. Responsibility is inherently attached to power, but until we recognize what power we already have, we continue to live in unconscious programming. We get stuck in the four energy patterns and resist learning new systems, blame the economy, resent our bosses, justify poor performance, and judge ourselves for not measuring up.

When people are clear about who they are and what they want, they don't waste time on drama. When people feel empowered, they do not resort to blaming others for their unhappiness. They take responsibility to ask for what they want, initiate change, stay with a difficult conversation, and look for solutions.

Between Responsibility and Choice

If taking responsibility means that you must first recognize choice, why is it so difficult to get people to recognize their choices? Two reasons come to mind: stubbornness and internal programming.

Let's look at stubbornness first. Remember the Drama Triangle? It stays in motion because of a need to be right, which in turn keeps people from looking inward to admit they were wrong and find solutions. This will prevent even the most brilliant person from seeing the choices they have. Some might refer to this need to be right as having an ego; however, status is one of our primary needs. If we feel threatened, this need surfaces in unproductive ways.

Any desire you have to be better than someone else, prove your point, argue, or outshine is going to be a problem when it comes to recognizing choice. Justifications like "I'm more educated," "I have seniority," or, "Because I said so" abound here. It doesn't matter what reason you manufacture; if you want to be right more than you want teamwork, you will make sure that you are—usually at the expense of alienating those around you.

If this doesn't sound like your problem, then perhaps you're unable to recognize choice because of programming. Science has revealed that we human beings are pretty much programmed by the time we are eight years old. The way we see the world and the way we interact and perceive are very much related to our past programming.

Until we can teach ourselves to think differently, the untrained mind runs the show. In terms of running your company, this means that you have to invest in some training for your staff if you want culture change. It goes without saying that as a leader, you are the most responsible one on board. You can't be an irresponsible boss and somehow manage to garner responsible behavior from your staff. Until everyone recognizes the signs of unconscious behavior, you won't be able to simply tell employees to change their attitudes and magically have it happen.

You Can't Change What You Don't Recognize

Until your employees recognize their choices, nothing much will change—because everyone is running on autopilot. But reprogramming is not as difficult as it sounds. Simply teaching people to identify the four energy patterns and making them aware of these principles for about a month would most likely put the wheels of change in motion. Remember, what you focus on expands. If you want to improve in any area, concentrate on improvement.

One of my favorite books is *The Master Key System,* by Charles F. Haanel, which was originally published in 1912 and is now available in several recent editions. This book offers short, weekly lessons on how the subconscious and conscious mind work, and offers the following vital information on the importance of training: "Ease and perfection depend upon the degree in which we cease to depend upon the conscious mind" (Haanel 2007). Haanel is suggesting here that before you become competent in anything—whether it is running a chain saw, driving a car, or thinking productive thoughts—you have to use your conscious mind to program the desired behavior or thought pattern. This will allow it to become ingrained in your unconscious.

A while ago, I went through a process that tested my ability to reprogram my unconscious. I decided that I wanted to start using cloth shopping bags to help the environment. Since this wasn't something I'd do without having to think about it, I had to reprogram myself to make it a habit. I started by putting the cloth bags into my car so that I wouldn't have an excuse to get out of using them. Then, even if I entered the store and realized I'd left the bags in the car, I'd force myself to go back outside and get them. After a few times of doing this, I was in the habit of using them. I no longer had to think about it; it had become part of my unconscious.

Training is really nothing more than programming or reprogramming. It takes consistency to change an ingrained habit, whether that habit is how you drive your car or how you process information. That is why negativity breeds negativity; we are programmed to look for and experience drama. Changing this ingrained pattern to one of responsibility will impact your customer service, your teamwork, and ultimately, your bottom line.

Where Change Happens

But what happens if you do provide training that proves not to work so well? You have doubtless heard the saying, *you can lead a horse to water but you can't make him drink*. That is true of employees too. You can coerce, you can try a guilt trip, and you can threaten firing—but if the horse doesn't want to drink, all the training in the world will not work.

Before you institute training, there is another energy pattern that invites change and transformation, which I will introduce now.

The Fulcrum Point of Change

There is a place where lasting change happens, and it can't occur through force or resistance. You can't persuade or judge someone into being a better worker. Most of us, even very competent leaders, respond to resistance with more resistance. So while you can't manipulate change, you can create a tipping point where change happens. I refer to this moment as the *Fulcrum Point of Change*.

There is a place right before change—a kind of energy pattern—that opens the space for change. This pattern is called *willingness*; this is the Fulcrum Point of Change, and the antidote to resistance. When you learn how to move your people into a state of willingness, you will be amazed at the cooperation and flow that emerges. Once you learn the related concepts and the language, you'll see how this skill translates in both your personal and professional life.

The Magic Phrase

There's a magic phrase you can use to turn the situation around when a complainer comes to you in a state of resistance. When your own boss is angry and negative, you can use the magic phrase to get him back to a reasonable place of peace. When a client is opposing your price, you can open up a little space of consideration once you use the magic phrase.

The magic phrase is: "Are you willing?"

Since willingness is the Fulcrum Point of Change, nothing happens until there is willingness. The heels are dug in, the decision is made, and opposition pulls everything to a dead stop. Whenever you are stuck, there is a lack of willingness. It's a lot like what occurs when you're in the integrity gap—how your values and actions are not aligned. You are rowing in circles, never getting to where you say you want to go. You want to go to the island but are not willing to get into the boat.

You can use the magic phrase "Are you willing?" to help you decide which island you really want.

I recently spoke at a workshop on this topic. I was illustrating the point that if you aren't getting the results you want, you either aren't clear, aren't telling the truth, or aren't willing to do what is required.

I then asked the audience a personal question to help convey how this works: "What would you love to do but feel that you cannot do?"

A woman replied, "I would love to take ballroom dance lessons."

"That should be pretty easy," I said. "Are you willing to sign up for private dance lessons in the next two weeks?"

"Oh, my husband would croak," she answered. (Resistance in the form of blame.)

"Are you willing to let your husband croak?" I continued.

"Well, it's not really him. It's just that dance lessons are so expensive." (Now what's really stopping her is an inability to tell the truth.)

"Are you willing to spend the $65 per lesson to try it out?" I asked.

"No," she admitted. "But I still want to learn to dance." (This is the integrity gap: She wants to dance, but is not willing to spend the money.)

"Well, are you willing to take less expensive group lessons? They are only $10."

"I'm afraid I would be embarrassed. I'm so clumsy."

Can you predict what my next question was? "Are you willing to be clumsy in order to see if dance lessons are something you really want; or is this just a fantasy?"

I do not know if this woman ever took the dance lessons or not. My job as trainer was not to get her to take dance lessons. My role was to get her to align so that there was no more division.

Until we undergo this process, we sometimes lie to ourselves and others about what we want; justify why we can't have what we want; blame other people or circumstances for us not having what we want; then feel resentment toward our situation and judge ourselves for not having the courage to change the situation. This is nothing but resistance and a lack of awareness. You see, it didn't matter to me whether this woman decided to take dance lessons or not. It mattered that she gained clarity to either go to the island called "I don't want dance lessons" or go to the island called "dance lessons." Either way, she was going to have to be willing to release the desire, be embarrassed, or spend money.

The Fulcrum Point of Change involves finding the point of willingness that will align you with what you really want and allow movement again.

The Fulcrum Point of Change at Work

If you want to coach someone else out of resistance, make sure that you are coming from clean energy first. Don't take action if you are feeling resentful, or if you are judging yourself or someone else. Once you are starting from a solid place, then you can decide what action isn't working. For example: If you have a coworker who always leaves you a mess, simply ask (instead of blaming or complaining), "Larry, would you be willing to take this stack of papers off my desk and file them?"

The challenge will be to hold your tongue, and not go on and on. In this instance, you are the one who has to be willing to change the way you lead—and this willingness has to take place from one end or the other. That is when change happens.

Larry will either agree or offer resistance. If he resists, then you must be willing to find out why. Consider that there may be good reason—and now you get to find out why Larry keeps leaving you a mess.

Don't fall into the trap of resisting just because he does. Just keep releasing resistance, and you will see some movement.

"Yes, Larry, I can see why it is difficult to finish on time. Are you willing to stop a little earlier so that I can come back to a clean area?"

See how you acknowledged what is difficult for Larry but still asked for his cooperation? This is much more effective than saying, "Larry, quit making excuses and clean up your mess."

No matter what your leadership role—parent, supervisor, administrator, leader, or owner—guiding those you lead into acting on choice is the key to developing a responsible team. Listen for the patterns of blame, resentment, justification, or judgment anytime you are stuck. The people you lead must be willing before any change can occur. Telling someone how to be or act is not going to create lasting and positive change. You could say to your employee, "I want you to get a better attitude, and I want you to be a team player," but she won't know how to do this. She is just reacting from programming and unconsciousness outside of the understanding of responsibility. Because she does not understand how to be responsible, she is looking for a rescuer and will ask her boss to fix her problems. She does not realize she is wearing the ruby slippers. In leading others to responsible choice you show them that they have the power—and have had it all along.

Questions to Answer

1. What do we need to accept now that seems unacceptable?
2. Where is negativity showing up?
3. What are some possible ways to facilitate positive change?
4. What must we be willing to do to move forward?
5. What kind of training is needed to assist the team?

Learning Points

◆ You cannot facilitate lasting change until you accept what is.
◆ Resistance is the nonacceptance of what is.
◆ The brain is wired for negativity.
◆ The four energy patterns of resistance are blame, resentment, justification, and judgment.
◆ People make the same mistakes over and over again due to old programming.
◆ You need to train people to reprogram negative habits.
◆ Responsibility is the recognition of choice.
◆ The Fulcrum Point of Change is willingness.

Chapter 8

Become a Creator

Logic will get you from A to B.
Imagination will take you everywhere.

—Albert Einstein

Always seek out and encourage creative employees who see choices even in difficult times. A key distinction of a creator is someone who recognizes choice. Great employees are the ones who believe in free will.

Dr. Roy F. Baumeister, professor of psychology at Florida State University in Tallahassee, said in a letter to me on this subject that a belief in free will predicts better job performance. We are not arguing the point whether free will exists or not; we are discussing the belief that it's beneficial to act on it. What if there was one question you could ask during job interviews that would determine who would be a responsible worker?

My interpretation is that our belief in choice allows us to create a better workplace.

The Premise of Becoming a Creator Is This

The path to developing a great team and positive workplace is empowerment. Leaders must be able to develop other creators. Creators take responsibility and see opportunity. They don't blame the economy, another person, or a situation. They live life in the flow and from the field of possibilities. "Become a creator" is a fancy way of saying take responsibility.

According to *The Power of TED (The Empowerment Dynamic)* author David Emerald, creators concentrate on the outcomes they are committed to achieving. Rather than merely reacting to problems and focusing on what they don't want, they focus their vision on what they do want. Emerald claims that becoming a creator can definitely make a bottom-line difference for your business. One of his clients—the CEO of a technology services company—reported that they increased the pipeline of prospects four-fold and experienced a 32 percent growth over the previous year—during a period in which many competitors struggled or went out of business. The CEO attributed this growth to implementing TED and focusing everyone in the organization on becoming a creator.

Recognize Choice

In order to create, you have to first see yourself as a creator and be willing to recognize the choices that you have. For over a decade, I have been advocating a new definition of responsibility: the recognition of choice. The victim's mantra is "I had no other choice." Therefore, they blame, resent, justify, and judge instead of being part of the solution. Even training will fall on deaf ears if the people you're training don't believe in free will.

Are there power struggles, sarcasm, and rude behavior in your workplace? You can teach communication skills and personality theory until the cows come home, but self regulation won't occur until your staff learns to recognize choice. Old programming always takes over, and the victim is glad to have an excuse in claiming "That's just the way I am." The creator instead looks for the solutions, and then course-corrects along the path of change.

Why should a leader care about developing other creators? Self-regulation is important to human performance, not to mention avoiding a lawsuit or keeping a customer. In terms of your business, this means that when a customer is rude, a coworker is disrespectful, or an unwanted change occurs, the damage will be minimal with the person who can self-correct and self-regulate. Even when the boat springs a leak, the empowered and creative employee will choose instead of react. There will be a bigger gap between stimulus and response.

Exercising the power of conscious choice lets people feel more empowered; eventually, their programming is changed to a place where emotional intelligence and reacting with grace under fire is the norm rather than the exception.

The first part of being a creator is to recognize choice. Since leadership is about influencing others, a leader's number one duty is to be a role model and teach others about personal responsibility. That means helping others to step out of the old programming of the victim mode and recognize choice. After that, it's all about skills—the first of which is to listen.

Listen

Set some time aside just to listen to the conversations that are going on in your workplace. Chances are, you'll notice that a lot of time is being wasted complaining or revisiting the past. You will hear comments about who is wrong, why something won't work, why something is the way it is, or how it has always been. This "victim language" is the opposite of the more empowering and exciting "creator language." In the second type, you will hear conversations about options, choices, possibilities, collaboration, and problem solving.

Speak

Train yourself not only to listen for victim language but also to speak as a powerful creator. This requires you to clean up any unconscious patterns you may still have. Any time you hear negativity, you know there is a potential drama problem brewing. You can clear the negativity by being aware of any unconstructive thought patterns that take up space in your mind, and then making a commitment to taking responsibility for your language. Any time that you or your team members' language indicates a lack of choice, you have a red flag, a blind spot or opportunity.

There are some vital leadership skills you can use to empower your team. All of the following suggestions are made with the assumption that, as the leader, you are either already skilled in speaking as a creator or you are totally committed to improving any weak areas before expecting your staff to change.

Ask Good Questions

The better your questions, the more positive the influence you will have over your team. It has been said that the answer is in the question; in other words, we get what we ask for. For example, asking "Why do you always make the same mistake?" is a question that will give you an answer in the form of information or an excuse, but probably not a solution for positive change. However, asking something like "How can we avoid making that mistake again?" helps you to identify the problem and seeks a solution for positive change. While there is no denial that a mistake has been made, there is also no blame and no room for excuses.

The brain is designed to answer questions, so be careful what you ask it. If, for instance, you ask yourself "Why am I so incompetent?" your answer might be that you never finished college, you are unstable, and you are too stubborn to ask for help. And there's your answer. However, if you ask "What can I do to increase my competency on this project?" your brain can now say to you, "You can ask for some help; you can spend some time doing research; you can get enough rest so you are more alert." Asking the right question can make all the difference.

The point here is twofold: you must first gain the skill to ask the right questions when you speak to your staff, and you must also teach your staff how to ask the right questions to get different results. Make a game out of it. Practice on these questions to see if and how you can reframe them in a more positive light:

◆ Why did you fail to get your sales quota?
◆ When are we ever going to learn this new computer system?
◆ What are we going to do if they cut jobs?

Now let's look at some different ways to ask these questions:

◆ What can we do to raise your sales quota?
◆ How could we learn computer systems more quickly and have some fun while doing it? Or, who could we get to train us on the computer system so we can advance quickly?
◆ How can we find creative ways to ensure we keep all of our staff?

See the difference that a good question can make? The following three kinds of questions will help you empower your team and generate solutions:

◆ The *Responsibility* question: What are your choices?
◆ The *Vision* question: What do you want?
◆ The *Decisive* question: What are you committed to?

The Responsibility Question

There is one question that you need in your leadership toolbox that trumps all others because it helps you get your team members to recognize choice—and it's as simple as this: "What are your choices?"

When Betty comes to you complaining about Janet, your first question is "What are your choices?" When John begins making an excuse about his sales performance, your question is "What are your choices?" When you have to give Rhonda probation for her bullying behavior for which she shows some regret but still doesn't indicate that she's learned her lesson, your question is "What could have been your choice?"

If in any instance you hear "I didn't have a choice" or "I don't have any choices"—or if you hear any trace of blame, resentment, justification, or judgment, such as "I wouldn't have done that if she hadn't started it"—then you tell John, Betty, or Rhonda to think about it and come back tomorrow at two o'clock to talk about possible choices. Period.

Although you may be tempted to buy into their story or try to fix it for them, be patient instead. You must empower them to be responsible, and they can't do that until they recognize that they have a choice.

I am not suggesting they will love their choices, mind you; I'm simply saying that in order to expand their opportunities, they must first recognize their sense of responsibility by way of their choices. I'm also not saying that you can't be compassionate and offer some coaching later on. But you don't want to do this too soon; otherwise, it will be an instance in which you're rescuing a victim.

Try to see your employees as powerful, accountable individuals, and have good intentions for their improvement and transformation. And when they do come back to you the next day, reward them with praise. I promise you will see a shift in their demeanor, which is always an indicator that change has taken place.

The Vision Question

If the choice question does not work (or even if it does), there's another question to keep in your toolbox that will help you move forward instead of blabbing about what is not working: "What do you want?" Most people have no clue what they really want. If they knew, they wouldn't waste time on drama-centered talk. Instead, they would spend more time discussing what island they want to go to than talking about what is wrong with the island they are marooned on.

Talking about what you don't want does nothing but waste time. Unfortunately, most of us are guilty of focusing on what is not working. The question that eventually breaks that spell by bringing us out of drama and to a decision is "What do you want?" If you can detach from the need to rescue others from their drama, asking these questions can be quite entertaining—and can teach you a lot about others and yourself.

I was recently working with a committee to plan a program where I was going to be speaking. It didn't take long for the meeting to get out of hand and the complaining to commence. "The budget needs to stay small. We can only charge so much. The people we are inviting do not really care. There is too much work for this committee . . . blah blah blah."

I had to take a deep breath, because it was a challenge for me to keep my cool and not judge. So I used the decisive question: "What do you want?"

"Well, we still don't have a conference room, and I don't have time to call 10 places," and so on the answers went.

I took another deep breath and asked, "I understand the problems. My question is, *what do you want?*"

Once again the tangent continued. "Well, the reason we don't get people on the committee who have the resources is because. . . ."

"Wait a minute," I said. "Please, in one or two sentences, tell me what you want—and we can get started making that happen." This question was followed by utter silence—and a few dropped jaws.

If you can coach your team members to verbalize what they want, then you will help to facilitate positive change—not to mention save lots of time in eliminating unproductive storytelling.

Do Not Take the Bait

Please be aware of how easy it is to take the bait, in other words, to take part in arguing, making others feel guilty (persecution), rescuing by offering to do things you will regret later, and so on. Being a leader requires a lot of self-monitoring until your new programming kicks in and becomes automatic. The first thing you want to do when you hear negativity and complaining is to offer a solution; however, there's usually some element of resistance until the emotional component is managed.

Your second impulse might simply be to instruct team members to stop bickering and just do as you say. You may want to say something like "If you don't like it, find another place to work" or "No one else is complaining."

A third reaction is to leave the meeting, and then go blow off steam to your closest work confidant about how clueless your entire committee is. Taking this route is a sure sign that you have taken the bait.

All these reactions only keep the drama alive when you want to be building creators instead. You have to be incredibly clear with your team members so that you do not get pulled into their negativity and claims that everything is impossible. Here is how: The minute you hear even the slightest trace of negativity, resistance, or drama, take a breath and separate yourself mentally. Consider the following creative visual; it can make the drama less intense while helping you keep your sense of humor. Visualize yourself as a fish and your coworkers' negativity as a huge hook with a juicy worm. You might want to picture something like a large slice of cheesecake, or anything else that would be tempting for you to bite onto. This will change your experience; it will be as if you are watching a movie instead of playing the starring role. You have effectively separated yourself from the drama.

If your awareness has not developed enough to notice the hook, you will take the bait. Remember how I told you in Principle 1 that the person with clarity navigates the ship? As a leader, you have to be so clear that you don't get pulled into the complaints, excuses, and regrets. Asking the right question can get everyone back on track.

As soon as you notice an increased amount of storytelling and complaining among your staff, you want to ask: "What do you want?" Once a person is able to articulate exactly what she wants, you'll be able to frame the "Are you willing?" question we discussed earlier. You can then state exactly what is going to be required to fulfill the commitment.

Do Not Be Fooled

Despite the power it can have to turn certain situations around, this question does not always bring instant results. There is some lag time—so be prepared. You may hear some version of a hopeless question like "I want to know why this always happens to me." Don't be fooled by this kind of fake answer, because that's not what you were looking for. That answer is a trap to bait the hook and complain. Always be prepared for more storytelling—how someone did someone wrong, why the system needs to change, or why something is "not my job." Just keep coming back to the central question by applying the broken record technique. Continue to ask, "What is it that you want?" Do not add another two cents to the conversation until that question has been answered honestly and appropriately.

"I Want a Raise!"

How many times have you heard something along the lines of "What I want is a raise" or "What I want is a promotion that includes a corner office and a new title"? It's as if you are a genie in a bottle who can grant these requests without any effort on anyone else's part. Once again, you must teach them to be responsible and to become creators by helping them articulate in one sentence what they want, why they are qualified, and how moving them up in the company adds value to the overall mission and vision. You can't get to the island if you can't name the island or at least point in the general direction.

The Decisive Question

Once you have helped your employees to recognize choice and have asked for what they want, you now have to test their commitment. Just because someone is clear on what they want does not mean that they'll necessarily do what is required to get it. Remember the chapter about the Fulcrum Point of Change? Nothing will happen until someone is willing. A lack of willingness in the form of excuses, blame, or resistance is a signal that you should revert back to the first question: "What are your choices?" Sometimes there's still a lack of responsibility—or an unwillingness to do what is required—even though someone claims to want something.

For example, I was coaching someone who wanted to start a business as a consultant but had all kinds of excuses as to why it wouldn't happen—one of which was "I haven't finished my master's degree." Even though this woman knew what she wanted, she was consumed with assumptions about what was required. In her situation, her training, and skill set were such that I knew she could offer her services as a consultant—even if she just did it part time to get her feet wet. I also knew that not having a master's degree could not hold her back if she was confident in what she was going to teach.

Your next question in circumstances such as these—when someone knows what she wants and you see her potential—should be "What are you committed to?" This question is very aligned with the question we talked about in the chapter on the Fulcrum Point of Change. Willingness and commitment go hand in hand. When a person is committed, she is willing to do what it takes to get the promotion or raise. However, you must first help this person to develop the list of criteria. This is a critical way that you can have a hand in the process of advancing people in your company.

Provide Structure and Processes for Advancement

Most organizations have some structure or process that allows for a raise or promotion if certain requirements are met. However, I have worked with many small companies or private practices that really don't seem to have any criteria. This setup makes it easy for owners and managers to grant these kinds of advancements based on a fear of losing the staff member who has been there the longest or knows the most about a particular part of the company. No employee should ever have that kind of power over you. You must find creative ways to recognize and reward those who step up to the plate and do what is required—and beyond. Remember—you have the power to set the tone of what kind of staff you want to attract into your business.

I recently met Donald Babb, one of the founders of Citizens Memorial Hospital in Bolivar, Missouri. Babb told me that when he was starting the hospital, he kept getting job applicants who wanted a distinguished title and substantial salary; however, none of these applicants had the skills required to do the job. One employee was so persistent that Babb finally told her that he would hire her—if she would get the training required to fulfill the obligations that the job required.

Do you see how Babb gave the job applicant the power to choose? She knew what she wanted, but he had to test her level of commitment and willingness to do what was required. Since she was willing to complete the training and fulfill the obligation necessary, her work ethic was rewarded with employment.

It's also critical to remember that new employment, job titles, and enhanced income naturally come with new responsibilities. When one of your staff members, employees, or crew members is getting ready for a promotion, make sure that he understands what he needs to do in order to live up to the new title. A job description with tasks and responsibilities written out should do the trick.

Work can be something that feeds our souls if we promote engagement and get people excited about what is possible.

The next step to becoming a workplace of creators is to constantly open the field of possibility. This will be challenging at first because our brains crave certainty. However, they also crave novelty—and the solution to offering this kind of novelty means doing something that I call *opening the field of possibility*.

Open the Field of Possibility

Nothing new is ever manifested until the field of possibilities is opened. Take, for example, my experience of working on the lines of a factory floor for more than 20 years. Until I considered that something else might be possible, there was no option for change. I lived based on the assumption that this was as good as it could get. Although I had hopes, I never made any conscious endeavors to change the situation—because I didn't believe it was even possible. It finally became a possibility when I asked myself, "What if I could actually do something different and make a living from it?"

Think of the technological advances that have taken place in just the last 30 to 50 years. The very first cell phone was offered by Motorola Dyna-Tac in 1973. It was $9 \times 5 \times 1.75$ inches and 2.5 pounds. You could use it for 35 minutes, and the only features it offered were talk, listen, and dial. Would anyone have imagined in 1973 that there would someday be something called an iPhone that would fit in your pocket, allow you to play games, access the Internet, and talk to someone across the globe using Skype without even having to pay a long distance fee?

Someone has to ask "What if?" in order for something new to emerge. However, most of the instances in which we ask this question are couched in negative ways. What if it doesn't work? What if he says no? What if we lose our biggest client? While looking toward the future with these pessimistic "What if?" scenarios can be helpful for developing plan B or measuring your risks, there is another way to use "What if?" If you find yourself stuck in your business, unable to meet your sales quota, or incapable of seeing any way out of a bad situation—then it's time to open the field of possibility by asking "What if?" in a more positive way.

- ◆ What if we can create a miracle today?
- ◆ What if there is a way to avoid a layoff?
- ◆ What if there is something that we're not seeing?
- ◆ What if we need to rethink our target market?
- ◆ What if we can turn this around in two weeks?
- ◆ What if we can afford the new equipment?
- ◆ What if it turns out to be easier than we think?
- ◆ What if we could start working better as a team?

The question "What if?" is in direct opposition to the statement, "I already know . . ." Any time you hear yourself or anyone else start a sentence with "I already know," use the "What if?" statement to open the field of possibility. In fact, I hope you are motivated just reading the "What if?" sentences above. Any time you are stuck, play this game to expand your mind as much as you can.

The What If? Game

If you really want to have fun with the "What if" game, incorporate it into one of your informal meetings or staff development sessions. Let one person start with a "What if?" and then encourage the next person to add to the previous question. You will have a few laughs and open your mind to countless possibilities. Select two or three "What ifs?" to focus on for the week. One of the reasons that negativity and resistance pervade our workplaces is because we have forgotten the joy of creativity. We often get stuck in what is and do not consider the possibilities of what could be. When you are acting as a leader-creator, you can move mountains. People want to be engaged and part of something bigger. The phrase "What if?" will do wonders to open the field of possibilities. Until something is considered, it is not really possible to look for evidence that will support a given opportunity.

Looking for Evidence

In your role as head creator, you'll want to help your team look for evidence of what you want to draw to your business. You do this by setting an intention—in other words, planting a seed of what is to come. When leaders show that a given task or goal is indeed possible—and make it sound easy to achieve—team members will come up with ideas and resources you never dreamed possible.

In fact, you probably do this all the time without even realizing it. For example, think about how you educate your sales team to know what to look for in a target market. Once they're aware of what to look and listen for, they can then take action. You can use this same tool to motivate your team to work together.

Remember earlier when we talked about your reticular activating system? The RAS is that part of your brain that helps you to pay attention to that which you want to attract. We use this part of our brain all the time without knowing it.

Whatever you want is around you. You just have to learn how to see the evidence. If there is a type of client you want for your business, one experiment you can do is to brainstorm about the signs, the very subtle signs that indicate a particular person might be your client. Have each person write down one sign they want to look for and put this sign on an index card. Tell your staff to write down any evidence they see that this type of client is out there.

This exercise works on many levels to help increase your awareness around any area where you need to step up your game, attract new clients, or gain new insights.

Suppose you try to do these exercises but you get no engagement. Your staff sits there at the meeting with their arms crossed and mouths closed. This kind of reaction indicates that there's some foundational work you need to do first in terms of building trust. A negative climate isn't going to elicit any cooperation from a one-time team meeting whose goal is to find evidence of better things to come. Creating a new climate of creators is a journey—an ongoing process that can vary in length, depending on many variables.

Acknowledge the Good

People are motivated by success. The best way to acknowledge people is by recognizing their qualities and talents. Make a list of the key people you need to involve in helping you implement change, and list one admirable quality or talent that each of these people possesses. For example—Sarah is very detailed and accurate, Jason always has a positive outlook and is very charismatic and articulate, and Renee is the best at solving customer problems. Address each team member individually to compliment them on these traits and ask for advice. "Sarah, you are so detailed and accurate. I've been watching you and I'm impressed. I am looking at ways we can evolve to make next year the best year yet. I can see how improving accuracy among everyone is going to save us $10,000 next year—so I want your ideas on how we might be able to do this. Are you willing to come to me with some ideas by Thursday the 23rd? All I ask is that you take some notes and be conscious of areas of opportunity."

Now you have planted a seed for the task at hand in Sarah's head and made her feel good about herself in the process. You do the same thing one-on-one with those whom you want to engage. The process is to uncover their best traits and abilities, call them into the office, compliment them on these, and ask for their ideas on a given project by a certain date.

These conversations need not be longer than 15 minutes. When Sarah, Jason, and Renee come to you, compile their written ideas and schedule a team meeting with the entire staff. You could do four per week for two months and have a substantial amount of buy-in before you even start to implement change.

Create a Vision
After the first two months of gathering data and holding one-on-one meetings, schedule a team gathering for which you create an agenda with three items. The first item on the agenda should be to thank everyone for the ideas they contributed. Second, you'll want to give a report of the suggestions. The third step should be to brainstorm with the group to create a vision of what could be.

There are thousands of ways to get your team engaged in the vision. You may need to actually schedule a retreat to take this further, depending on the size of your company, your goals, and the amount of change you are going through. However, whatever your company's size and objectives, you will have success if you can lay a foundation and get everyone involved in the vision. People support what they help to create.

What if all their ideas are crazy? It is important that you learn how to self-monitor and keep from rolling your eyes when Janet suggests something absurd, or when Ken's contribution indicates just how clueless he really is. You have to remain open. You already know you aren't going to be able to implement every idea and that not all ideas are even feasible. The goal here isn't to implement every single suggestion you hear, it's to transform your team into creators. Using these methods promotes trust and engagement. You might even be surprised at how much your employees know and are willing to contribute if they're just given the chance.

Once you create a vision you can live with, construct some goals and a method of reporting back on reaching these goals. Make sure you have identified what is required to achieve each one. Do not set yourself up for failure. Make sure you know the time requirements, staffing requirements, sacrifices, and resources you need to move forward.

Create Structure and Measurement

You need to measure your results to keep everyone motivated and make the needed adjustments. Your team will lose motivation if you develop a grand, exciting vision—with no way of knowing you are getting there. Make your vision measurable and keep the progress visible in the break room or accessible on a computer. You can see the big island to which you are heading, and everyone is in the boat rowing toward it. Keep the vision in sight so that you always know you're getting closer. Make sure to update your team with news, changes, and goals reached.

So, how do you keep your employees engaged and rowing harder and smarter during the process? We all know what the beginning is like; it's exciting and everyone is motivated. Then you get stuck in that gap that we talked about earlier. One of the best ways to get their engagement is to increase their status.

Develop Their Expertise

As we discussed earlier, human beings have one primary desire once their basic needs are met: to keep or raise their status. Change—whether in the form of a merger, downsizing, or simply hiring new people—always invites a little drama in the form of complaining, excuses, and regrets. The reason? People worry about losing their status.

That is perhaps one of the many reasons it might be difficult to get people to speak up at meetings—they often think that it might be too risky, they might be judged, or others might disagree. Scared people do not make the best decisions; those who are just trying to hold on to their jobs are not really engaged. They are just there for a paycheck.

One thing you can do to really ramp up engagement is to make these people experts in your company. This requires implementing some fairly entrepreneurial ideas—some of which might need to be altered if you work in a highly regulated practice such as accounting, insurance, or banking. However, these methods can work brilliantly in privately owned practices ranging from spas to plastic surgery clinics, to carpet cleaners, to car repair shops, to landscaping companies.

The concept of increasing your employees' expertise is grounded in the notion that since everyone is good at something, why not make each person a subject matter expert within your business?

For example—let's say that you run a private practice plastic surgery clinic and have an esthetician on board; let's call her Janie. What if every time a patient came in for a visit, you gave the client an article that Janie had written featuring her photo? The article might provide information about the five ways to look 10 years younger by visiting an esthetician. It could be short and concise with simple tips and valuable content. You have now positioned Janie as an expert, and you have a relationship-building tool to give to her potential clients.

The same approach could work for a landscaping company. You might put a picture of Jim, one of your top landscapers, on a tips sheet full of advice about how to prune bushes in the fall. Mail these out at the end of summer along with Jim's contact information and details about the services he provides.

If you've already found a reason this won't work, then go back and read the chapter on releasing resistance. You may be tempted to say, "What if Jim quits and I'm stuck with all this customized promotional material?" Well, if Jim quits, simply replace his picture with one of his replacement. Worrying about whether the employees you develop will leave puts you in a victim mind-set. Any time you spend cultivating their careers allows them to bring additional revenue to your company. Giving them this sense of accomplishment will likely make them even more loyal to you.

Has your brain already said, "Janie is not a writer; that would just take too long"? If so, there's always the option of getting a good ghostwriter—someone who can interview Janie and write a short article in her voice. An artist can create a template for future articles, and turn these articles into PDFs that you can send via e-mail or attach to your Web-based newsletter.

Let's face it; you probably invest just as much in these activities as you would in hiring an advertising firm—a tactic that might not really be working. What could happen if everyone in your practice, company, or organization made a commitment based on their shared vision and sense of contribution? Make your people the stars and invest in their expertise. They have the knowledge and ability to do the basic work; you can always hire other people to write and polish the promotional materials while still highlighting the real experts who serve your clients.

Your experts do not always have to be those who are in sales or who meet with the public. You can create internal experts as well. Let's say, for instance, that Judy is the organizational guru in your company. Put Judy in charge of maintaining the standard operational manual. Have her present her updated methods at regular meetings. If Paul is a great teacher, give him a title as certified trainer—and give him a bonus check every time he trains a new hire. If your company is large enough, you can even put Paul in charge of creating a system to train the trainer. If Stephanie is creative and particularly computer savvy, find a way for her to create updates to post on Twitter and other social networking sites, or put her in charge of updating the company blog.

There are thousands of ideas to engage people and get their commitment, even if what you are asking them to do does not immediately equal advancement. When I was a factory line worker, I didn't have any status other than some seniority. This is actually a fairly big deal in labor-type jobs, partly because there is not much room for advancement. One day, I got an opportunity to present part of the safety program. Granted, the topics on which I was presenting—new safety technology, OSHA regulations, and why you should wear earplugs and goggles—is pretty dry material, but I got permission to spice it up. I got prizes to give away for people who got involved. I managed to get a few people to participate in a skit, and I created a quiz to see if people understood the material. I got to create the program any way I wanted—as long as it covered the most important topics.

I have to admit, I did worry about the presentation a little. I didn't know if my coworkers would see me as someone who was trying to "suck up" to management, or if management would criticize me for being too creative on such a serious subject. My secret hope was that I would somehow be seen. I wanted to contribute in a way that used my gifts and natural talents—and I wanted to be acknowledged for it. In addition, I wanted other opportunities.

And much to my delight—I did receive acknowledgement from my coworkers. They gave me encouraging words like "You could be a professional speaker" and "That is the best safety presentation we have ever had." However, the company's management didn't say a word. Not only was there no acknowl-edgement; they didn't even notice. They were just doing what was mandatory—holding a safety meeting—and now they had one more thing to check off of their already packed to-do list.

This was not necessarily a bad thing. I am actually thankful that management did not see my value immediately. I probably would have stayed at the company longer and might have not built the career that I have today. But I learned an important lesson from being on the bottom rung: Everyone has talents—even if they don't know it, and even if their talents aren't noticed or appreciated by their organization's management. Everyone wants to be seen for their potential and everyone wants to be acknowledged.

The manager or leader who can do this is a genius and has the power to build creators.

Celebrate Success

My final advice in developing a team of creators is to constantly celebrate success. Your team contributes to the success of the company in some way every single day, week, and month. It is important that you find ways to commemorate both small and large achievements. Though people are motivated to be suc-cessful, they lose that motivation when they're met with an "it's never enough" mind-set. No one wants to constantly row without a resting place.

Part of your job as a leader is to create a sense of completion. If your island is 5,000 miles away, stop on the island that is 500 miles away and celebrate. Let your employees lie in the hammock for a minute and sip the coconut juice. Then they will be motivated by their success to get to the next island 500 miles away. Don't make the mistake of thinking you will save time if you keep cracking the whip and skipping the celebration. They will lose vision faster than you do.

Owners and leaders frequently experience frustration because of their own impatience. So many worry that their team members only seem to be concerned about the seat cushion in the boat, while you have your eyes on the island. This is too significant of a gap to ignore. You have to look forward, look down, look forward—then celebrate. In order to keep your employees motivated, they have to be updated, kept in the loop, and allowed to enjoy the fruits of their labor.

Questions to Answer

1. What kind of negativity shows up in my workplace?
2. Am I a good role model for personal responsibility?
3. Where do I fail to use empowering language?
4. What do we need to measure that we are not currently measuring?
5. Whom do I need to recognize and acknowledge?
6. How can I help to develop my staff's expertise?
7. What is needed to develop more of a creator mind-set in our workplace?

Learning Points

- Good leaders self-regulate.
- Responsibility is the recognition of choice.
- The better the question, the better the answer.
- Ask for what you want, not what you don't want.
- Don't take the bait to negative invitations.
- Willingness is the shift right before change (or willingness is the fulcrum point of change).
- "What if?" opens new possibilities.
- What you want is around you—just look for evidence.
- People are motivated by success so celebrate regularly.

Conclusion
No Complaints, No Excuses, No Regrets

Your priorities, business concerns, and opinion of your workplace are influenced by your position in the boat. The captain is concerned with getting to the treasure chest on the island, the leader is concerned with having the rowers paddle harder and faster, and the rower is concerned with getting a more comfortable seat cushion.

Imagine the impact that would result from being able to see a bigger picture that includes everyone's interests, while enabling you to facilitate positive change—even through turbulent waters. No matter how difficult the current economic situation, how dismal things may seem, and how much drama your workplace endures, there is a higher truth: There are opportunities all around you. We miss seeing all of these chances when we view our organization with tunnel vision.

We can only see what we already believe to be true. This tendency is known in psychology as *confirmation bias*. (For an explanation, see www.skepdic.com/confirmbias.html). Frequently, even when new evidence of possibility occurs, we humans simply revert to our default view to confirm what we already to believe to be true. Our beliefs about what is, who we are, and what is possible keep us from thinking outside of the box to contribute in bigger ways. As a result, we wait for permission to experience success and for others to meet our needs. We are like Dorothy in *The Wizard of Oz*—waiting for someone else to change or notice us, or for some opportunity that eludes us. We aren't aware that all along, *we* have the power to achieve these things within us. This phenomenon plays out in the way employees approach their work and thus miss opportunities to play a bigger role that would benefit the company.

I saw a powerful example of this firsthand when I was facilitating a workshop on thinking outside the box. I met Marsha, a part-time worker for an environmental disaster clean-up company. All Marsha could think about was how to convince her boss to make her a full-time employee. In the meantime, I saw several people give Marsha ideas about ways to network her company and ways to partner that she didn't recognize as possibilities. "I don't know if we offer these services," was often her reply.

Marsha asked me directly—how do I convince my boss to make me a full-time staff member? I explained that she had to try to see things from her boss's point of view. I encouraged her to approach her boss every time she saw an opportunity and inquire about ways to turn these ideas into revenue or more clients.

"But I'm a very linear thinker," she replied. "I'm not really used to networking, thinking out of the box, and looking for opportunity. I have an accounting background, and I'm not naturally creative." (Can you see the resistance?)

"You can learn," I explained. "Just keep asking yourself: How do I become such a value to my company that my boss can't live without me? Every time you have an idea, show your boss how that idea could lead to your organization attaining more customers. Every time you network, let your boss know how your solid relationship-building abilities led to new getting clients. Use your accounting skills to show the boss where the company is losing money, instead of using your accounting skills as an excuse for not being creative."

Marsha was concerned with getting a great seat cushion and moving to a better position on the boat. A shift in her mind-set could help her get that new cushion (going full-time) if she provided enough value. I suspect both Marsha and her boss could benefit by asking a different question.

What if, no matter what your role or position, you constantly asked yourself the question: "How can I provide value?" The brain works to answer any question you give it. Imagine the impact on teamwork, communication, customer service, and eventually the bottom line if you consistently make this inquiry.

We generally lose momentum in at least one of the top three principles—clarity, relationships, and resistance—and in one or more of the other five principles in the Stop Your Drama Methodology.

Clarity

There will always be some chaos as a company grows; however, chaos is not the real problem. Recovering quickly and regaining clarity is the key to overcoming any commotion. When companies fail to walk the talk, the fog always rolls in and morale goes down. There is always a lack of clarity in some area wherever there is drama. Therefore, to eliminate drama, you must increase clarity and align your walk with your talk.

The Gap

Most of life is lived right in the gap, the space between where you are and where you want to be. If you do not know what is really required for the journey, or if you do not give your team the right resources, a substantial amount of drama will ensue. To keep morale high, know what is required, communicate the expectations, and give your team the resources they need to succeed. Shorten the gap by celebrating small successes so that your employees remain engaged and motivated.

Truth

Denial never solves the problem; pretending that there's no leak in the boat does not keep water from rushing in. To increase trust, you must eliminate exaggerations, recognize that there may be more to the situation than is immediately visible, and substantiate your claims with solid facts.

Reinvention

It's critical to keep developing yourself and to embrace personal change and growth. The way you see yourself impacts your leadership style. If you are acting out of sync with your values, realign your beliefs and your actions to make your word golden. You want others to see you as a leader—not because it's your title but because it's who you are.

Relationships

Without other people, you would not have a reason to exist—as a person or as a company. You cannot claim success without receiving help from others. Focus on building mutually rewarding relationships and you will not only decrease turnover and increase loyalty, you will also have a lot of fun.

Energy

Everything in life is comprised of energy. You owe it to yourself to learn how to master your energy and increase your awareness about energy's impact on performance. Negativity leads to exhaustion and suppresses the immune system, and working without sufficient recovery increases the chances for mistakes. To increase your own personal performance, master your energy and require rejuvenation of both yourself and others.

Resistance

All drama has an element of resistance, the nonacceptance of what is. Don't waste time on what went wrong, who is at fault, and why something didn't happen as planned. Remember: the Fulcrum Point of Change is always willingness. If you are seeking positive change that seems to be eluding you, ask yourself what you (or your team) have not been willing to do—or what you have refused to give up.

Creator

A creator mind-set is grounded in personal responsibility. If you want to hire good employees, look for individuals who take responsibility for their own success. To help others adopt a creator orientation, help them to recognize their choices—because you can't act responsibly if you believe there are no choices.

The eight principles in this book work in harmony with each other. For example, wherever you find a lack of clarity (Principle 1, Clear the

Fog), you will probably find an area where you need to tell yourself the truth (Principle 3, Tell Yourself the Truth). When you have a big argument with a coworker (Principle 5, Stop Relationship Drama), one of you will likely dig your heels in the sand, causing the project to suffer (Principle 7, Release Resistance). If you work too long and become physically exhausted, you may end up having a mental meltdown (Principle 6, Master Your Energy), and eventually this negativity will flow into your relationships (Principle 5, Stop Relationship Drama). Then you may jump to conclusions and make assumptions (Principle 3, Tell Yourself the Truth). You get the picture.

Do you need to memorize these eight principles and work them in a linear fashion? Of course not. Simply pick an area that resonates with you and make a few shifts. I suggest starting with clarity, relationships, or resistance, because all drama has at least one of these components—often all three.

Let's say, for example, that you had a significant amount of relationship drama in your workplace—a lot of blaming, finger pointing, and victim-persecutor behaviors. Upon investigation, you realize that your employees need some additional resources to make their work easier. You also realize that they are working long hours without breaks. Simply instituting time for rejuvenation (Principle 6, Master Your Energy), and providing the needed resources (Principle 2, Identify the Gap), could create a much needed improvement.

When you alter just one area, everything else in your work life starts to change. When I was in a personal transition between leaving a job of 21 years and before embarking on a professional journey, there was a very large gap between who I was and who I wanted to be. I began with a shift in which I started to see both my boss and myself differently. In effect, this shift increased my clarity and helped me to step into a new and bigger truth—eventually leading me into the career I enjoy today.

Transformation always happens on the inside first. This concept is difficult for some people to understand—especially those who like to take action and do not realize that inner work can be even more strenuous than physical labor. This is often why simply learning a new communication skill does not work if there is no internal modification to support the skill. Although there are many portals of change, mere words and actions are rendered powerless without a change in your mind-set, intention, or heart.

The challenge is to release the old ways of thinking that have held you back, and to see a bigger vision. We must listen to each other and learn from each other. I believe in the philosophy offered by Great Place to Work Institute: Any company can be a great place to work, and better workplaces lead to a better society.

The drama—what happens—is an unavoidable part of life. Every individual and company will experience obstacles, sometimes even chaos when undergoing considerable transformations. In fact, it may even seem like the biggest disasters strike right as you are in the midst of a deadline, a big transition, or facing a big decision. Despite the fact that this book is called *Stop Workplace Drama*, we all know the reality: As long as you are living on this earth, you will experience some obstacles to your peace and prosperity.

But drama is not really the problem. The amount of time you stay in the drama—and the effort you put toward it—is the problem. Complaints, excuses, and regrets only serve to keep the drama alive. We complain when we believe that we're powerless—when we blame someone or something else for our discomfort, unhappiness, or failure. However, even when you are at the mercy of some unfortunate circumstance or unfair action, you still have a say in what happens. If you want to lead from your power, you must assume responsibility for the one thing you can truly be responsible for: the way you represent yourself, and who you are at your core. You either decide to live with what is, or become creative and find a way to accept or shift the situation.

An excuse is just a thought that keeps you stuck—your own resistance to success. It lives in sayings like "It's too hard," "It may not pay off," "I'm too old," "They may not understand," "Because of my past, it is just not possible."

Any time you are really stuck, ask yourself what excuses keep you from moving forward. Most of us make excuses on a regular basis without even noticing.

The reason I didn't return your call is because I was too busy.

I would have been on time but the traffic was horrible.

Every excuse is simply one more indicator that you are letting outside circumstances control your life. Excuses strip us of personal power. I ask myself on a regular basis, "Where could I be without that excuse?" Try to ask yourself this question once in awhile; you will see that a self-awareness exercise like this one helps pinpoint places where you get stuck in the old story instead of reinventing and stepping into a new truth.

Regret is often the result of too many excuses. Fail to be responsive one too many times (even though you were busy), and you lose a customer. Show up late one too many times, and you lose credibility with your peers.

Regrets also come from reacting instead of responding, failing to think ahead, and from doing what you want to do now without recognizing how it may negatively impact your future. When you are clear about your core values, and you are more committed to the discipline of living congruently, you will find that you have fewer regrets. There is no more room for a temper tantrum, rude behavior, impatience, interrupting, or any activity that keeps you out of integrity with yourself, your employees, and your boss. When your actions align with what you say is important, you will be living more intentionally.

So, the next time you experience drama, ask yourself these questions: Where am I unclear? What is my relationship issue? Where am I resisting? Train yourself to ask these each time you experience the chaos of change, the urge to retaliate, the desire to win an argument, or the thought that you simply can't go on.

There is no reason to deny or be afraid of the drama—or even your own drama. Embrace what drama has to teach you about yourself, your values, and your opportunities for growth.

My wish for you is that you can use the ideas presented in this book to develop yourself, so you can live from your highest vision, inspire others through your leadership, and experience peace and prosperity.

Resources

Books

Allen, James. *As a Man Thinketh*. New York: Penguin, 2008.

Bruce, Anne. *Discover True North: A 4-Week Approach to Ignite Your Passion and Activate Your Potential*. New York: McGraw Hill, 2004.

Carbonara, Scott. *Firsthand Lessons, Secondhand Dogs: Living, Laboring, Learning . . . and Letting Go*. Naperville, IL: Scott Carbonara, 2010.

Childre, Doc, and Bruce Cryer. *From Chaos to Coherence: The Power to Change Performance*. Boston: Butterworth Heinemann, 2000.

Covey, Steven M. R. *The Speed of Trust: The One Thing that Changes Everything*. New York: Free Press, a division of Simon & Schuster, 2006.

Covey, Stephen R. *The 7 Habits of Highly Effective People: Powerful Lessons in Personal Change*. New York: Fireside, 1989.

Daniels, David, MD, and Virginia Price PhD. The *Essential Enneagram: The Definitive Personality Test and Self-Discovery Guide*. New York: Harper Collins, 2009.

Doniger, Wendy. *Splitting the Difference*. Chicago: University of Chicago Press, 1999.

Emerald, David. *Power of TED: The Empowerment Dynamic*. Washington: Polaris Publishing, 2006.

Glenn, Sam. *A Kick in the Attitude: An Energizing Approach to Recharge Your Team, Work, and Life*. Hoboken, NJ: John Wiley & Sons, Inc., 2010.

Godin, Seth. The *Dip: A Little Book that Teaches You When to Quit and When to Stick*. New York: Penguin Group, 2007.

Gordon, Jon. *The Energy Bus: 10 Rules to Fuel Your Life, Work, and Team with Positive Energy*. Hoboken, NJ: John Wiley & Sons, Inc., 2007.

Haanel, Charles. *The Master Key System*. Lake Hamilton, FL: Media One Publishing, 2007.

Hanson, Rick, PhD, and Richard Mendius, MD. *Buddha's Brain: The Practical Neuroscience of Happiness, Love and Wisdom*. Oakland, CA: New Harbinger Publications, 2009.

Hsieh, Tony. *Delivering Happiness: A Path to Profits, Passion and Purpose*. New York: Business Press, Hachette Book Group, 2010.

Kashdan, Todd. *Curious?: Discover the Missing Ingredient to a Fulfilling Life*. New York: William Morrow, 2009.

Lencioni, Patrick. *The Five Dysfunctions of a Team: A Leadership Fable*. San Francisco, CA: Jossey Bass. 2002.

Levering, Frank, and Wanda Urbanska. *Moving to a Small Town: A Guidebook to Moving form Urban to Rural America*. New York: Simon & Schuster, 1996.

Loehr, Jim and Tony Schwartz. *The Power of Full Engagement: Managing Energy, Not Time, Is the Key to High Performance and Personal Renewal*. New York: Free Press, 2003.

Patterson, Kerry, Joseph Grenny, Ron McMillan, and Al Switzler. *Crucial Conversations: Tools for Talking When Stakes Are High*. New York: McGraw Hill, 2002.

Ruiz, Don Miguel, MD. *The Four Agreements*. San Rafael, CA: Amber Allen Publishing, 1997.

Rock, David. *Your Brain at Work: Strategies for Overcoming Distraction, Regaining Focus, and Working Smarter All Day Long*. New York: Harper Collins, 2009.

Rogers, John, and Peter McWilliams. *Do It! Let's Get Off Our Buts*. Los Angeles: Prelude Press, 1991.

Sharma, Robin. *The Leader Who Had No Title: A Modern Fable on Real Success in Business and Life*. New York: Free Press, 2010.

Simon, David, MD. *Free to Love, Free to Heal: Heal Your Body by Healing Your Emotions*. Carlsbad, CA: Chopra Press, 2009.

Tolle, Eckhart. *A New Earth: Awakening to Your Life's Purpose*. New York: Penguin Group, 2006.

Tolle, Eckhart. The *Power of Now: A Guide to Spiritual Enlightenment*. Novato, CA: New World Library, 2004.

Tracy, Brian. *Change Your Thinking, Change Your Life: How to Unlock Your Full Potential for Success and Achievement*. Hoboken, NJ: John Wiley & Sons, Inc., 2003.

Walsch, Neale Donald. *Conversations with God: An Uncommon Dialogue*. New York: Putnam, 1996.

Zukav, Gary, and Linda Francis. *Mind of the Soul*. New York: Free Press, 2003.

Periodicals

Godfrey, Jocelyn. "Mac Anderson, On Goal Setting, Failing Forward, and Dancing in the Rain," *Attitude Digest*, Winter 2010.

Maney, Kevin. "SAS Workers Won When Greed Lost" *USA Today*, April 21, 2004.

Rock, David. "The Neuroscience of Mindfulness: Simply Put, with No Religious Overtones." *Psychology Today* (October 11, 2009), www.psychologytoday.com/blog/your-brain-work/200910/the-neuroscience-mindfulness.

Sirota, D., Mischkind L. A., and Meltzer, M. I. "Stop Demotivating your Employees." *Harvard Management Update* (January 2006).

Interviews

Cathy Demers, interview by Marlene Chism on "Setting Magnetic Goals," June 13, 2010.

David Daniels, MD, interview by Marlene Chism on Attitude Builders teleseminar, "The Essential Enneagram," June 18, 2010. www.attitudebuilders.com.

David Simon, MD, interview by Marlene Chism on Attitude Builders teleseminar, "Free to Love, Free to Heal," February 12, 2010. www.attitudebuilders.com.

Rick Hanson, interview by Marlene Chism on Attitude Builders teleseminar, "Stress Proof Your Brain," January 22, 2010. www .attitudebuilders.com.

Web Resources

Levering, Robert. (1996). *Employability and Trust*, Conference Board Meeting Chicago 12, September 1996. Retrieved April 12, 2006 from www.greatplacetowork.com.

About the Author

Marlene Chism is a dynamic business and motivational speaker and communications consultant who has the unique ability to reach across the boundaries of many types of audiences, from Fortune 500 executives, entrepreneurs, and business leaders to employees on the front lines. Marlene challenges and engages her audiences, inspiring them to "be more of who they really are, have more peace and prosperity, and do more of what really matters." She is a philosopher and a dynamic storyteller with the ability to take complex subjects and universal principles and make them immediately applicable.

Marlene is the founder of Stop Your Drama Methodology, an eight-part process that engages managers and employees with the tools to clear the fog, recognize their choices, change communication dynamics, and navigate toward change. Marlene combines universal principles with sound business practices to bridge the inner and outer game of success. She also knows firsthand what it means to reinvent. For more than 20 years, Marlene worked on the lines of a factory floor before quitting her blue-collar job to build a business as a consultant, trainer, and professional speaker.

Marlene is also a seasoned and dynamic radio guest or host, columnist, and expert consultant. She is known for her thought-provoking yet down to earth practicality, her sharp wit, and fun-loving humor.

To schedule an interview with Marlene, or for other press requests, please contact:

The toll free number is 1-888-434-9085
The local Springfield, Missouri, number is 417-831-1799
Or e-mail marlenechism@mchsi.com
Web sites:
www.stopworkplacedrama.com
www.marlenechism.com

Index

Stop Workplace Drama Resources
www.stopworkplacedrama.com

Join the Book Club For FREE!

Congratulations! Since you purchased the book, *Stop Workplace Drama*, you are invited to join the free book club which includes many valuable resources to help you improve personal effectiveness, live from your purpose, and increase productivity.

Videos ▶ Articles ▶ Book Club Forum ▶ Other Surprises

One Attitude Builders Lesson including an MP3 Audio and Learning Guide

Premium Level Membership for Leaders

The premium level membership is designed for trainers, managers, administrators and other leaders committed to developing their own leadership skills and growing other leaders. Added benefits include the managers' mastermind forum where you can leverage your knowledge by networking. You will have private, members-only access to:

—Staff development videos

—Instructions on how to develop your staff on a limited budget

—Managers' mastermind forum

—Special Report: *7 Ways to Reduce Workplace Drama*

—Six-pack of Attitude Builders interviews with authors, experts, and transformational leaders

—Learning guides and training exercises

—Personal development library with articles and MP3 audios

—Professional development library with articles and MP3 audios

Other Resources

www.attitudebuilders.com

www.marlenechism.com

www.stopyourdrama.com